KU-796-341

To my good Friend -
Dr Gardner.
Don.

22·5·54·

Mr Jones, Meet The Master

Peter Marshall.

Mr Jones,
Meet The Master

Sermons & Prayers

of

PETER MARSHALL

LONDON : PETER DAVIES

FIRST PUBLISHED 1954

Printed in Great Britain for Peter Davies Ltd
by The Leagrave Press Ltd., Luton and London

To Our Ain Mother Janet

PREFACE

PRINTED SERMONS are often as uninteresting as warmed-over potatoes. This is because they are designed to be heard, and are dependent on the preacher's personality for much of their effectiveness.

In the pages which follow, these difficulties have been largely surmounted by the use of an unusual format. Peter Marshall always preached with a complete manuscript before him. These sermons have been set up just as his manuscripts were typed.

Grateful acknowledgment is made to Dr Trevor Mordecai, formerly pastor of the First Presbyterian Church of Birmingham, Alabama, who first suggested this form to Dr Marshall twenty years ago.

Originally intended for ease in reading, the style eventually became an integral part of Peter Marshall's work. It adapted itself to his vivid imagination and strong poetic streak.

On the printed page it conveys much of the force of his personality, making articulate, almost audible, the written word. We believe that this style will add much to your reading enjoyment.

CONTENTS

Here Is Peter Marshall

I HEARD PETER MARSHALL preach and pray before I met him. Tall, with broad shoulders, his physique told of the years spent playing football and working in a steel mill. Sandy, curly hair—now a bit darker—and a burr to his r's spoke of his native Scotland. He gave the impression of irrepressible vitality and burning conviction.

Later, one warm May night we were both scheduled to speak on a Prohibition programme. The evening did not do much for Prohibition, because Georgia promptly and decisively went wet, but it did launch our romance.

The zest with which Peter preached was characteristic of the way he did everything from bowling to following the fortunes of the Washington baseball team. He worked hard, and he relaxed hard. Because he took Christ with him into his fun, young people loved to be with him, and, somehow, through sharing with him a fishing trip or an evening of chess, got a clearer glimpse of their Lord.

Dr Marshall loved games and played to win. To many friends he was known as "The Great Game Player", soon shortened to "The G. G. P". Upholding this reputation was very serious business indeed, though he worked at it with gaiety often bordering on hilarity. For some reason, it was always he who kept the scores, with the same meticulous neatness with which he kept his desk drawers, his finances, or his garden borders.

He had no use for long-faced Christians. The Christ he knew was a red-blooded Christ, and he was perfectly sure He didn't want namby-pamby disciples. This was illustrated by the evenings he spent at Washington's Presbyterian Home for the Aged. The Master he took with him was the Christ of the wedding feast who knew how to laugh and enjoy good fellowship. Beginning with a worship service, Dr Marshall usually ended at the piano, playing and singing anything from "Rock of Ages" to "Annie Laurie", from "The Old Rugged Cross" to the rollicking "Road to the Isles". He was not above delighting his white-haired hostesses with the gay "Laird o' Cockpen", "I'm Tickled to Death I'm Single", or even "O You Beautiful Doll".

Along with Dr Marshall's love of fun and companionship, there was always an odd boyish shyness. He was genuinely and deeply humble, but because this was not the pseudo pardon-me-for-living kind, people did not always recognize it as such.

At thirty-five, when he came to Washington to take the pastorate of the historic old New York Avenue Presbyterian Church, he said he was scared to death—and he was. A picture in my possession, taken in the pulpit by the Washington *Star* at that time, amply proves the point. Always he felt inadequate for the tasks to which God called him, but because he knew God had called him, he also knew he would get the help he needed.

Publishers often asked him to let them publish a book of his sermons. He would never even consider it. Once he answered: "I wouldn't think of it. There are enough second-rate books on the market already. I've no intention of adding more".

No one was more surprised than he when he was offered the Chaplainship of the United States Senate. He was in the yard pruning bushes when Senator Kenneth Wherry telephoned. Upon being asked if he would consider taking this post, he was astonished and said immediately, "No, I couldn't". But when Senator Wherry insisted, he agreed to pray about it and let him know. "I wouldn't think of allowing my name even to be considered, unless God definitely gives me a green light", he said.

Our assurance then that this was part of God's plan for his life has been substantiated, for not only did he come to mean much to the conscientious and overworked men of the United States Senate, but his new duties gave him an outlet for his deep patriotism and love for his adopted country.

The Senators, the visitors in the gallery, the page-boys, indeed the country as a whole, came to look forward to those terse, punchy prayers. Never will those who heard it forget the briefest of all, that of January 6th, 1948: "Our Father", he prayed, "who art Lord of heaven and of all the earth, Thou knowest the difficulties these men have to face and the grave decisions they must make. Have mercy upon them. For Jesus' sake, Amen". As Dr Marshall turned to go, Senator Vandenberg leaned over, smiled broadly, and whispered, "Now I know just how a condemned man feels".

Here, too, he felt his inadequacy. Once he actually pleaded: "Our Father, let not my unworthiness stand between Thee and the Members of this Body as we join in prayer. Hear not the voice that speaks, but listen to the yearnings of the hearts now open before Thee."

It was in the pulpit that the mantle of true greatness fell upon him. In keeping with his Scottish background, he always wore a robe, but never a clerical collar. From the Invocation to the Benediction of any service he conducted, people were immediately aware of the genuineness of what he was doing. He despised sham or pretence or what he called "the ministerial tone".

11

He worshipped along with his congregation. When he prayed, he was asking for pardon and peace and strength for himself, and so other people felt that he was voicing their own deepest needs.

He prayed about whatever was on his mind and heart. We were amused that sometimes this included the weather. It may have been inconsequential to us, but it was terribly important to him. He never became acclimated to our heat. He almost had a complex on the subject of America's torrid summers. The summer before we were married, his letters were half love letters and half lurid descriptions of how he was suffering as Atlanta's temperature rose. To those of us who knew all this, his prayers about the weather sounded strangely like rationalization. "O God", he would say, "we give Thee thanks for the beauty of this day. We know that it takes brilliant sunshine to ripen the grain and to make more beautiful the gardens which Thou hast planted and watered."

Dr Marshall's congregation always marvelled at his reading of the Scriptures. He could take the most difficult Pauline passage and read it with such understanding and lucidity that it sprang into life. What few people knew was that he had mastered the art of reading aloud when, as a boy, sitting before the fire in the long winter evenings, he had read the Bible hours at a time to his blind grandmother.

Dr Marshall's art in the pulpit was an unlearned art. All the tricks of great oratory, as well as the actor's skill, he employed unconsciously. He had the poet's feeling for descriptive words. Occasionally he would let himself go on the description of a sunset or the hills of Scotland. From these oratorical ventures he acquired the nickname of Twittering-birds Marshall from the four fellow ministers with whom he lunched on Fridays. One of these ministers once remarked wryly, "He has the language to gild the lily and pin ruffles on the stars".

His diction was almost perfect. A university speech professor advised his students to listen to either Orson Welles or Peter Marshall, if they wanted to hear perfect diction.

Like all great evangelical preachers down through the ages, Dr Marshall said nothing new, but he said it in a new way. The huge congregations which regularly packed the church and overflowed into downstairs rooms were gripped anew by the gospel.

An Army officer, admittedly thoroughly pagan, came to church only out of deference to his host and hostess. He left saying, "If I heard that preacher often, I'd have to change my way of life—that's all".

A business man who had not been inside a church for years finally yielded to his wife's pleading and came down to New York Avenue one Sunday. At the close of the service he walked out on to the sidewalk, his eyes filled with tears. "That's my preacher", he said. "Why did I wait so long to come? I'll never miss him again", and he never did.

None of this was surprising to those who heard Dr Marshall regularly. They had grown used to hearing this man who "laid it on the line" in picturesque style, with all the enthusiasm of a little boy who had just made the most exciting discovery in the world and couldn't wait to share it with everyone who would listen. They had grown used to seeing sagging balconies and two lines, four abreast, waiting Sunday after Sunday for admission.

There had to be some relief, however, from the pressure of crowds and the public eye. This Peter found at home. To him, his home was his castle, the one place where he could relax utterly. Here he resented the intrusion of business. His church office and his home were kept entirely separate. All business, even the making of engagements, was done from his study at the church. Our home reflected his taste. On the selection of most things we had equal say, but when it came to the choice of pictures, somehow I never had a chance. The boy who had grown up near the Firth of Forth, and who at fourteen had run away to join the Royal Navy, never got over his passion for the sea. So we ended up with four seascapes in the living-room, two large ones in the dining-room, five in our bedroom, and a few others scattered throughout the house.

His taste in colour was just as decided. Fortunately, we were equally fond of blue. Otherwise, I should have been most miserable. Once in an evening sermon he confided to the congregation, "I hope I shall live to see the day when we mere men can enjoy colour more than we do, and when we can dress in whatever colours we please. There is no good reason why we should not dress in robin's egg blue suits, cerise ties, and lemon-coloured socks, if we want to".

He was always most appreciative of all the details that went into creating a home. Often his blessing before a meal would be: "Father, we thank Thee for the loving hands that prepared this food". Sometimes, though, he was not quite so generous in his praise. I have seen him sit down, look at what was before him, grin at me and say: "Catherine, I think you'd better thank God for this. I don't want to be a hypocrite".

When in a jovial mood, he liked to revert to Scottish expressions. When our little boy talked too much, he was *just a blather*. When he stumbled over the furniture, he was a *glaikit lump*. When our cocker begged at the table, he was a *wee gutsie dug*.

These Doric expressions were reminiscent of Dr Marshall's mother. She is by no means the lavender-and-old-lace type. At eighty she still does all her own housework, and her blue eyes sparkle with merriment at her own jokes.

14

During the last war at the height of the blitz, when the British were expecting German invasion hourly, she wrote, "I just dare Jerry to try to invade our house. I keep my shovel and my poker handy, and *I'll dunt the breith oot of 'em and skelp 'em* alive".

Several years ago we visited her in Scotland. Peter was the kind of sailor who was still relishing his food when the boat was listing so that all movable objects were on the floor sliding from one side to the other. I had a fine voyage admiring the ceiling of our stateroom.

While we were in Scotland, I asked Mother Janet for her recipe for that British delicacy, steak and kidney pie. I took it down just as she gave it to me. "*First, ye inquire at the Flesher's for two puir wee sheep's kidneys and a half pound o' steak, cut 'em up, brown the pieces in a wee saucepan wi' a wee pat o' butter——*"

Because Peter had had so few possessions when he was growing up, he was especially appreciative of all lovely things. He was a collector at heart. Antique glass started out as my hobby and ended up his. He would collect almost anything—bone china, etchings, stamps, books, rose bushes, or old pomade lids to frame. In the summer, on Cape Cod, he enjoyed the auctions. Once he came home bringing a desk, a Windsor chair, a table, two blue vases, and a brass woodholder. He would spend hours refinishing a piece of furniture or putting wax on a maple table. Our cottage was his pride and joy. Soon after we acquired it, he himself painted the green shutters blue.

Since part of God's plan for him was coming to this country, one whole side of his personality would never have been developed had he missed that Master Plan and stayed in Scotland. He had a depth of feeling for his adopted country which few native-born Americans ever have. This sprang partly from his passionate conviction about

America's God-appointed destiny and partly from his overflowing gratitude for all this country had done for him.

During the last war while in a railroad dining-car, he was seated opposite a soldier just returned from overseas. The ribbons on the soldier's breast not only attracted Dr Marshall's attention, but somehow stirred his imagination. He was suddenly so overwhelmed with gratitude for what the soldier and his comrades had done for him, that as he rose to go—on a sudden impulse—he leaned over, and indicating the service ribbons said, "Pardon me, but I just want to say thank you". Then a little embarrassed himself, he hurried out of the car, but not before he had seen a look on the soldier's face that made him wonder if he had ever heard such a thing before.

So much did Dr Marshall love to preach, so sure was he that this was the thing God had designed him to do, that it was hard for him to turn down engagements. Though he had a rugged constitution—for Scotland's rigorous climate does not pamper—his strength did not quite equal his enthusiasm. On the morning of March 31, 1946, he collapsed in the pulpit with an attack of coronary thrombosis. After a few months of convalescence, he launched into the most vigorous and productive period of his life. Then on January 25, 1949, at 8.15 in the morning, quietly he slipped through those phantom walls that separate this life from the next. We had only five hours' warning.

Peter was well prepared for such an eventuality, though it never for a minute dimmed his zest for life or made him slow down. He had thought a lot about death. Even in the very early years of his ministry he had preached many sermons on immortality. His thinking and writing on the subject comprise an original contribution at a point where such a contribution is sorely needed.

"When the clock strikes for me", he had said, "I shall go,

not one minute early, and not one minute late. Until then, there is nothing to fear. I know that the promises of God are true, for they have been fulfilled in my life, time and time again. Jesus still teaches and guides and protects and heals and comforts, and still wins our complete trust and our love.

"The measure of a life, after all, is not its duration, but its donation. How much will you be missed?"

Those of us who stood helplessly by—often with uneasy minds and wistful hearts—watching him pack his threescore years and ten into a scanty forty-six, know just what he meant.

CATHERINE MARSHALL

June 1949,
Washington, D.C.

Publishers' Note: In 1952 we published Mrs Marshall's biography of her husband under the title of A MAN CALLED PETER.

17

Prayer

Our Father in Heaven, give us the long view of our work and our world.

Help us to see that it is better to fail in a cause that will ultimately succeed than to succeed in a cause that will ultimately fail. . . . .

May Thy will be done here, and may Thy programme be carried out, above party and personality, beyond time and circumstance, for the good of America and the peace of the world. Through Jesus Christ our Lord. AMEN.

I am growing more and more aware that all too often we preachers aim at nothing and hit it.

From THE REAL THING

Some Things I Know

E VERY MAN in public life
    every speaker who takes the rostrum
    every preacher who mounts the pulpit
has certain reticences.

The modern preacher, particularly, hesitates to inject personalities into his preaching.
He is reticent about using illustrations out of his own experience or that of his congregation.

But the apostolic preachers and writers observed no such restraints.
Their sermons were full of their own experiences.

"What we have seen and heard, declare we unto you", they said.
They never tired of telling what the Lord had done for them . . .
    what they had been before . . .
      what they were now . . .
and in the simple telling, there was power—sheer power.

This power that had made them different, they said, was available to anyone who would believe.
Sins could be forgiven; Christ could come into human life
    to change natures and dispositions . . .
      to change moods and temperaments . . .

to banish fear and worry . . .
to remove shame and guilt . . .
to provide a new dynamic, a new purpose in life . . .
a new joy and a peace that nothing could destroy.

It was exciting news.
People listened to it.
They did not always agree with the apostles, or like what
they said. Sometimes there were riots, and bloodshed.
Riots . . . or regenerations.
Never . . . just apathy or indifference.

We modern Christians are remarkably frank about some
things and strangely reticent about others.
The trouble is that we are frank about the things that were
better left unspoken or are too trivial to matter,
and silent about the only things worth discussing and
sharing.

We do not seem to have any great faith these days—
in God and His power . . .
in His ability to salvage wrecked lives . . .
to change human nature . . .
to take away our mood of futility . . .
to guide our decisions . . .
We seem to have little faith in the availability of the Holy
Spirit—the Helper—in our daily lives.

We have no great convictions
no great passions
no great causes.

Two World Wars have convinced us that there really is

not anything worth dying for, and we are not sure that there
is anything worth living for.

Perhaps it is because of this desperate need for a new dynamic in human life that, more than ever before, we need the
testimony of those who have made spiritual discoveries.
Lately I have had a feeling of compulsion to tell a bit of my
own story and the convictions growing out of it.
I do not know why it was laid on my heart to do so.
I do not need to know.
For did not Christ say, "Go home and tell thy friends what
great things the Lord hath done for thee"?

When a person can say, "I know *Whom* I have believed" . . .
when he can say: "I know that prayer changes things",
he has done more to instil faith in other hearts than all the
arguments since the world began.

What do I know out of the crucible of my own experience?

I know that Christ is alive,
    and personal
  and real, and closer than we think.
I have met Him.
I have felt His presence.

I have seen the changes He can make in me . . .
    in lifting a mood,
      in taking away despair or frustration or hopelessness,
        in breaking down my stubborn will,
      in melting my pride,
    in getting me to do the right thing when I preferred to
do the wrong thing.

23

I know that I now belong to Him.
I am His child.
I know that I am a Christian.

Now upon this point, there need be, and indeed can be no
doubt or hesitation.
One either is a Christian—or one is not.
   One either is a believer—or one is not.
There is no middle ground of compromise or indecision.

When someone asks you if you are married, there is no
hedging or uncertainty.
You either are—or you are not.
You are in no doubt concerning your citizenship.
You either are a citizen of the land in which you live, or
you are not.
There is no possibility of equivocation.

So, it is not humility or piety to say that you are
   "trying to be a Christian" . . .
      or that you "hope you are a Christian".
You either are—or you are not.

Either you have given your life to Christ and asked Him to
be your Master, or you are still trying to run your own life.
Either you have promised to obey Christ in all things
or self, ego, is still at the centre and at the helm.
It is one or the other.

I know that Christ has "taken me on"—that I am now His
child and His responsibility, and that He will make all the
changes necessary in me, now and through eternity, until
I am what He wants me to be.

I know that without Him I am absolutely helpless to do
what I know I ought to do, to change my own character,
    or my habits
  or my disposition.
But I also know that He can change them.
He can help me to overcome any weakness or failure by
getting to the root of the trouble.

He may dig deep,
and there may have to be some spiritual surgery.
For instance—maybe in looking at ourselves and life, we
come to the conclusion that we ought to be different at
some point.

We long to be a little kinder to people.
    We know that we should be more tolerant,
      more understanding,
    more interested in other people
and their problems.

Perhaps we have a fiery temper that breaks out like forked
lightning, and we say and do things of which we are afterwards ashamed.
So we pray for more grace, for more patience, more understanding.
But that's not the real trouble.
It lies deeper than that.

What we really need is for Christ to perform some spiritual
surgery on us; to cut away the stubborn pride which makes
us want to domineer other people and order them about.
Secretly we want to be dictators and bullies.
It is this ego which must be cut away.

But although I have never been more aware of my own inadequacies, I have never been so aware of the adequacy of Christ.

He can do with me what I cannot do, and change what I am unable to change—*and He will.*

The only thing which delays this, is my own unwillingness to be changed.

There is in each of us just enough self-will to make us think as we repeat the Lord's Prayer:

"Thy will be done—(in other people)
Thy kingdom come—(but not just yet)."

I know that Christ is interested in every detail of my daily life and of yours.

And why not?

If He has numbered the hairs of our heads . . .

if He notes the sparrow's fall . . .

shall He not care about what we do every day and how we do it?

Most of us simply refuse to believe how practical God is.

He is ready to tell us what to say in an important conversation.

He is ready to help us make the right decision in a difficult choice.

He is ready to guide the hand of the surgeon,

and the scissors of the housewife.

He is ready to give new strength to the tired servant standing over the kitchen sink.

*   *   *   *

He led me from Scotland to the United States of America

twenty years ago, when I had no idea of coming here.
I had first thought when I gave my life to the Lord, that I
would be going to China as a missionary.

Doors were closed, and doors were opened, and in His own
good time, God led me to America for the purpose of
entering the ministry.
I prayed for three weeks for the answer that led me to
apply for an immigrant's visa.

The weeks passed, and I could not understand why God
did not give me a plain answer.
I was impatient.

Then one Sunday afternoon the answer came.
I could never describe to anyone how I knew, but there was
no mistaking it.
One moment I was walking along undecided—and the
next moment, I *knew* that it was God's will for me to leave
Scotland.

I don't think I could describe it any more accurately.
But those of you who have had experience in prayer will
understand.

Even after this decision was made, I had to wait a year and
a half for a visa.

I had no idea what lay before me, or how or where or when
I would enter the ministry.
That I was willing to leave to Him, who had led me thus
far on my way.

I prefer to say as little as possible about the first five months

I spent in this country, in New Jersey.
I worked hard for long hours.
  I dug ditches.
    I wielded spade and shovel.
      I was unemployed.
I had three different jobs in five months,
but no contact with any church, no indication of any
possibility of achieving my ambition and following the call.

Then came a letter from Birmingham, Alabama, offering
me a position with a newspaper there.
I felt, at once, that this might be the second step in my
guidance.
So I made it a matter of prayer.
  Should I go South?
    Was this the way into the ministry?

Within a week I knew that it was.
My prayers were answered definitely and without doubt.
I borrowed money, and made my way to Birmingham.
There I found friends.

I met Dr Trevor Mordecai of the First Presbyterian Church,
to whom I owe more than I shall ever be able to repay.
The first time he saw me, he felt that there was a deep
significance in our meeting, and that somehow it was laid
upon him to help me.

He knew, before I told him, that I sought to enter the
ministry, and he promised to help.

The events of the next few weeks were so amazing and so
exciting that I know they sound almost unbelievable.

Within the space of a few short weeks, I had joined the
First Presbyterian Church,
    had been recommended by the Session as a candidate for
    the gospel ministry,
        had spoken at prayer meeting,
            had been elected president of the young people's
            league,
                had become interested in the Boy Scouts of that
                church,
and had been asked to become the teacher of the Men's
Bible Class.

All of this took only a few short weeks.
It was agreed, however, that since the seminaries were
already in session, it would be well for me to wait until the
following year, since I could use the time to become
acclimated
    to make friends
        and to gain some valuable experience.

It was a happy and a busy year.
My salary with the newspaper was very small, and I was
unable to save anything.

When the time came around for me to enter the seminary,
some of my friends were quite concerned about how my
theological education could possibly be financed, since I
still had no money.

Under the spell of all the wonderful things that had already
happened to me, I believed implicitly that a way would be
provided, although I could not imagine how.

Call it naïve if you will, I believed the Lord would provide a way . . . and so He did.

Just before I left for seminary, the Men's Bible Class assured me of their interest in my going, and that they would follow me through with their prayers.

Understanding the difficulties I might encounter in seminary and in order that I could devote myself wholly to my preparation, they pledged themselves to send me a specified sum every month while I was in seminary.

This they did for two years.
Since I supplied a church in my senior year, I was able to graduate without debt, save that obligation to the Men's Bible Class of the Old First Church, which I can never repay.

My experience with God's guidance did not end there, for in each of my first two pastorates in Georgia I had clear and unmistakable indications as to where the Lord wanted me to go.

This historic old New York Avenue Presbyterian Church in Washington then called me, and I prayed about the matter for two or three weeks.
I simply could not feel that it was God's will for me to come and so I declined the call.

Eight months later, the second call arrived, but this time there were factors that made it clear that it was the will of God.
I accepted the call for that reason.
I did not want to leave Atlanta.
I was very happy there, and from every human consideration I wanted to stay.

I came to Washington believing sincerely that that was God's will for me, that He had specific work here that He wanted me to do.
Such has been the case.

Thus I can say to you, I know that God can and will supply our physical needs, whatever they may be,
" For your Heavenly Father knoweth that ye have need of all these things".

I know that God is interested in the practical details of our daily lives, for the Bible is filled with assurance and illustrations.
Furthermore, so many people have found these promises to be true—and can say, as I say, that God can be trusted.

I have been out of work because of strikes and depressions.
I know what it is to be unemployed and to look for a job.
I know what it is to be without a home in a strange land.
I know what it is to have no money at all, for I have walked down Broadway, looking for work, with two cents in my pocket.

Yes, I have at times been without many things, but never without the One Who cared.
All through my life, God has supplied all my needs, richly, generously, far beyond anything I could have asked or dreamed. I know that God wants and expects us, His children, to ask Him
for guidance,
for protection
and for help
in a hundred details every day.

C

I know that He is far more willing to do things for us than
we are to ask Him.
And that is the great mystery—why, knowing what we do
about God's power and God's willingness to help, why we
keep on struggling ourselves . . .
trying to work out things our own way, when He could
save us all the anxiety, do it better and easier.

I believe our pretended, pathetic self-sufficiency saddens
God.
He longs to help us, but we won't let Him. We refuse to
ask Him.

I know that when I take time to talk to God and to obey the
promptings of the Holy Spirit—those little nudges on the
inside—I feel alive . . .
    and life is joyous and a great adventure.
I know that when I neglect these things, I begin to feel
tired, and half-dead. I become miserable,
    irritable,
        full of frustration.
My work becomes complicated and a great burden, instead
of a joy.

I know that it is to my immediate self-interest to obey
Jesus—both what He has told me to do as it is written in
the New Testament, and what He tells me to do day by day
through the Holy Spirit.

I have no spectacular story to tell, but I do know that more
than once my life has been spared, when others around me
have been taken.
I have felt in my own experience the invisible messengers
of God, and I believe in the presence and in the ministry

of guardian angels.

When the clock strikes for me, I shall go—not one moment
early, and not one moment late.
Until then, there is nothing to fear.
I know that the promises of God are true,
for they have been fulfilled in my own life, time and time
again.

Jesus still teaches
             and guides
          and protects
       and heals
    and comforts
   and still wins our complete trust and our love.

These things I know.
And in my story, Peter Marshall is not glorified, but the
Lord. As a matter of fact, as I think back over the evidences
of the Lord's guidance in my own life, I feel ashamed that
my faith is not a more radiant, contagious thing.

God's hand has very evidently been upon me, and I should
be a better man because of it.

Surely if God has done so much for me, how much more
will he do for you?
If His goodness and mercy have followed me all the days
of my life, will they not also follow you?
Should you not be encouraged to believe that these same
things and many more can happen to you?

These days of doubts
   and fears

suspicions
   and unbeliefs call for a positive faith
and a steady witness.

The situation in which we find ourselves in our national
life and as individuals demands a clear note and a confident
faith. We need people who are willing to stand up and be
counted people who are not afraid to say, "Yes, I am a
Christian".

Yet we Christians have almost lost the art of religious
conversation. We have not mastered the art of leaving
behind all pious terminology and speaking naturally and
spontaneously about the things we most surely believe.
We are not to argue about Christianity; that is the most
futile
   the most useless
   and the most devastating of our temptations.
We cannot prove the things of the spirit by reason . . .
not because they are unreasonable—but because they are
beyond reason.

The things of the spirit are matters of perception—not of
proof.
As Paul tells us in his First Corinthians' letter, ". . . the
things of the spirit of God . . . are spiritually discerned".
                                        (1st Corinthians 2:14)

We do not argue, for example, about beauty in music
   in art
   or in poetry.
We recognise that in these realms, beauty is either appreci-
ated or it is not.

Can you imagine a musician trying to prove by argument
that a piece of music is glorious?
> Does the poet argue for his sonnet?
> > Or the artist for his picture?

We cannot prove the inspiration of the Bible by argument,
> nor the efficacy of prayer
> > nor the reality of God's guidance
> > > nor the power of God to change people's lives.

No—we must not argue about Christianity.
Christ does not expect us to.

All He asks us to do is to tell what we know, what we have
experienced.
He will do the rest.

Why are we so reluctant to tell even our friends, those
whom we know best, about Christ and to talk to them about
spiritual things . . .
> to discuss with them how to find God's will for their
> lives . . .
> > to help them to cultivate a prayer life?
Why are we so reluctant?

Perhaps it is because we are embarrassed to talk about
spiritual things.
We are afraid of ridicule.
We do not yet understand how normal a thing it is to know
God and to live our daily lives in fellowship with Him.

Many of us lack the fortitude to stand by our convictions.
We permit a few secular pagans in our office to silence us
entirely.

Most of us, I think, are silenced by reason of the fact that there are some things wrong in our own lives, and if we were to say too much about spiritual things we would be hypocrites, and our friends know it . . . and we know that they know it . . . and so we say nothing.

Therefore, it seems to me that before we can do what Christ asks us to do, we will have to set right some things that are wrong.

And *then* we will have something to say, and it will be so *real* to us and so *terribly important* that nothing else will matter.

We will go to our friends as Jesus told us, and we will tell them what we know of Him . . .
    what He has done for us . . .
    how He answered our prayers about this matter . . .
and how we reached a decision that was not only the right one, but the happiest one for all concerned . . .

And we will tell them how we found His guidance
    and how our own lives have been changed . . .

There is only one way to learn the art of religious conversation and that is to try it.
    You can't learn to fish by studying a book.
    You never swim until you get into the water.

"Go home to thy friends and tell them."
That's what Christ wants you to do.
He wants them to know that He is as adequate for life in our day as He was nineteen hundred years ago.

Suppose for a moment—suppose He is counting on you to tell them?

Prayer

O God our Father, history and experience have given us so many evidences of Thy guidance to nations and to individuals that we should not doubt Thy power or Thy willingness to direct us. Give us the faith to believe that when God wants us to do or not to do any particular thing, God finds a way of letting us know it.

May we not make it more difficult for Thee to guide us, but be willing to be led of Thee, that Thy will may be done in us and through us for the good of America and all mankind.

This we ask in Jesus' name. AMEN.

Church members in too many cases are like deep sea divers, encased in the suits designed for many fathoms deep, marching bravely to pull out plugs in bath tubs.

From PASTOR'S POSTSCRIPT

Disciples In Clay

I WONDER how you would like to be on an investigating committee. Apparently there are some people in Washington who enjoy that sort of thing.

Suppose you had been on such a committee nineteen hundred years ago, to inquire into the qualifications of those who sought to become disciples of Jesus. Suppose you had been one of a group with authority to examine the credentials of the men who presented themselves as candidates for discipleship. How would you have voted on them?

Let us imagine we were there on an examining board.

Here comes the first candidate.
He has just come up from the beach.
His fishing boat, drawn up on the pebbled shore has worn seats, patched sails, and the high rudder that is characteristic of Galilean fishing craft.

As you can judge from his appearance, he has just entered middle age.
But he is already bald, and the fringes of hair that remain are already grey.
His hands are rough and calloused.
His fingers are strong.
He smells of fish!

He is an uncouth person—not at all refined, or cultured, or educated.
Blustering
  blundering
    clumsy
      impulsive
he does not strike us as being material for the ministry.
Then, too, his age is against him.
Maybe he is too old.
Why, he is forty if he is a day.
Does not the ministry demand young men?

Not so, when we need medical attention.
We do not specify that the attending physician be in his late twenties. No, we don't want anyone practising on us!
Or when we find ourselves in legal trouble, we do not insist on retaining as our counsel the most recent graduate of the law school.

On the contrary, we seek someone with experience—someone who knows the ropes well.
If he happens to know a judge or two, so much the better.

But considering a minister, a preacher, we cannot ignore his age—and this man's age is against him.
His ideas will be very hard to change.
He will be stubborn
  set in his ways.

He is a rough man, and he has lived a rough life.
When provoked, he is liable to burst into profanity, and his vocabulary is lurid.

Can you imagine this big fisherman as a disciple of Jesus?

He would not be your choice, would he?
No, we'd better send Simon back to his nets.

The next candidates are brothers; they come in together.
They, too, like Simon Peter, are fishermen.

They come from the same village, from the same colony of
rough, strong men who work with their hands for a living.

But you are not going to hold that against them, are you?
Let no social snobbishness sway your judgment.
Remember the Lord Himself was a carpenter.
There is no shame in manual labour, and would it not be to
a preacher's advantage to know what it is to do manual
labour?
Would it not be excellent preparation for the ministry?

These two men are looking at you.
Their eyes are steady, accustomed to far distances.
They are good weather prophets.
A glance at the sky and a look at the lake, and they can tell
you what is brewing.

They know the signs of the sudden squalls that whistle
through the mountain passes and come screaming down to
make the water dangerous.

They, too, have strong hands and nimble fingers.
They make quite a team, these brothers.
They operate a boat in partnership, and they are very
successful. In fact, it is a mystery to their competitors
how they always manage to find the fish
    always catch more than the other boats

and how they manage to get better prices for their catch.
This naturally does not increase their popularity among the fishermen.

But it is chiefly their attitude that irritates the others.
They are not modest men.
They are boastful, and through cupped hands they like to shout taunts to the other fishermen hauling on their nets.
They have earned for themselves the nickname "the sons of thunder", because they are always rumbling about something.

The way they feel, they have little patience with people who cross them, and they would be inclined to call down fire from heaven to burn them up.
Get rid of objectors!
That's their motto.

They are ambitious men, and if the stories are true that are whispered about them, they have been brought up to believe that if you want anything in life grab it.
Their mother had taught them that to get on in the world you have to push.

They would want to be in the chief places.
They think they belong in front.
If they became disciples of Jesus, they would naturally want to be His chief lieutenants—one on His right hand and the other on His left.
If we took time to hear all the testimony from people who know them, our verdict would be unanimous that James and John would simply not do.

So let us pass on to the next candidate.
There is a wild gleam in his eyes—and no wonder.
He is a leader of the Underground.
He seems to be of the fanatical type, impatient and nervous.
See—he cannot keep his hands still—
   his fingers clench and unclench.

They itch to reach up and haul down the hated pennants of Rome that hang in desecration from the walls of old Jerusalem. His blood fairly boils when he is forced, by some clanking legionnaire, to make way on the pavement and step into the gutter.
He dreams of the day when the Kingdom shall be restored to Israel, and the promise of the sacred writings that when the Messiah comes He shall restore the Kingdom, is his meat and drink.
His eyes dance at the thought of the Messiah, at the head of a liberating army,
   driving the hated Romans into the sea.

Yes, from the hill country they would come, and from the cellars of the Holy City they would rise up to bring back the glories of David and of Solomon. He wants, more than life itself, to be a part of that glorious campaign.

But this young man might be too dangerous.
He is highly inflammable material.
He is likely to become violent, and his impatience will burn him up.
He is a great risk—a very great risk.
We could not take a chance on Judas.
   We dare not.

Notice how the ladies greet this next candidate.

He will have their vote right away.
We are all drawn to him, and the men, however grudgingly,
have to admit that he is handsome.
He walks with an easy grace.
There is nothing effeminate about him,
  but he is gentle
    refined
  every inch a gentleman.

Endowed with all the social graces, who could possibly
say a word against him?
His eyes are like limpid pools.
His smile melts your heart.
But when he starts the day, it is not to take up the tools of
his trade, for he has none.
It is not to yoke the oxen to work in the fields, for he never
soils his hands.
It is to wander off to day-dream.

He is a Ferdinand sort of man. He likes to smell the flowers.
He is an introvert—a dreamer.
But don't you know that the work of the Kingdom demands
extroverts—men who are interested in other people?
Don't you realize that it is not castles in the sky we pray for
—but the coming of the Kingdom of God upon this earth?
We have to pray for it—
  and work for it, too.

No, Nathaniel is a good man, everybody agrees, but he is
simply not the type we need.

We are not doing very well in selecting disciples, are we?
But think of the material we have to choose from.

Well, what about this fellow?
He, too, is a fisherman.
Let's not hold that against him.
If you are not a tradesman, or a farmer cultivating a bit of
land, dressing some fruit trees or tending grapes, if you have
no sheep or goats, there isn't much else for you to do but
fish.
For people have to eat, and fish is the best money crop in this
part of the country.

This man might have it in him to be a disciple.
He is not impulsive by any means.
He will not be swept off his feet.
He is very cautious, slow to convince.
He must have been born in some little Palestinian "Mis-
souri".
You have to show him.
He demands proof for everything.
He'll take nothing on faith.

Now, this twist of mind and character will always slow up
the work of any group to which he might belong.
He will be like the rusty little tramp steamer in the convoy.
He'll slow down the others to his own wheezy seven or
eight knots.
In fact, he has only two speeds, dead slow and stop.

Can you imagine him as a member of the apostolic band?
Always advocating delay.
"This is not the time", will be his theme song.
"Let's wait and see," will be his advice.

But the Kingdom is a venture of faith—not of doubt.
It is a matter of perception—not of proof.

45

How could Thomas possibly fit into that picture?

Now, if we were Jews living at the time the disciples were originally chosen, we would boo or hiss as this next candidate enters, for he is a Quisling.
He has sold out to the army of occupation and is collecting taxes for the Roman government.

Think of how the collaborators were regarded in Norway and in France, and you have some idea of the feeling that runs against this man.
Tax collectors are seldom the most popular men in any community, and this fellow is a racketeer to boot.

He has devised his own particular racket and it is making him many enemies and making him rich as well.

But that's not all.
He has a mind like an adding-machine.
He has been counting money all his life.
Money and evidences of wealth alone impress him.

That's bad enough, but there's worse to come.
He is a genealogist.
He is one of those men whose passion is family trees.
He will bore you with long recitals of the best families—
    where they came from
        whom they married
            how many children they had
                and whom they married and so on . . . and on.

Can you imagine a Quisling as a friend of Jesus,
    a statistician walking with the Carpenter from Nazareth,
    a man who had made a god of money?

No, Levi, or Matthew if you like, must be rejected.

What about this fellow Andrew?
Does anyone know about him?
I have heard it said that he has no personality—whatever
that means.

I know that he is Peter's brother, but I know of no good
reason why he should be chosen.

There are others still waiting—Bartholomew
        Thaddeus
    Philip and another James
  and a man called Simon from Canaan.
They are all interested in becoming disciples, but I know of
no particular reason why they should.
We would not vote for any of them.

Yet these are the very men whom Jesus chose to be His
disciples, that is, all except Nathaniel.
I simply included him because he is attractive and Jesus
liked him.

I feel sure you would not argue with me if I suggested that
these men had more influence on the course of human
history than any other dozen men who ever lived.

Each man was different.
As Dr Buttrick has commented
"Philip looks before he leaps;
Peter leaps before he looks".[1]
Thomas was a dogged unbeliever until the last minute.
Judas sought regeneration through revolution, instead of
revolution through regeneration.

James and John wanted to get rid of people who differed with them, instead of getting rid of the differences, so that they could get the people.

Had you and I been members of any investigating committee we would have rejected every one of them.
Yet Jesus chose them.
Why?

Mark tells us in his Gospel that Jesus chose them "*that they should be with him* and that he might send them forth to preach, And to have power to heal sicknesses, and to cast out devils".

Well, they were with Him for three years, in intimacy of fellowship.
They walked with Him, they lived with Him.
They heard His incomparable parables.
They listened to every sermon He ever preached.

They saw with their own eyes each one of His wonderful miracles.
They saw the blind receive their sight, the lame throw away their crutches.
They saw withered limbs become straight and strong.
They even saw the dead raised to newness of life.

All these things they saw and heard.
Yet these things did not change these men.
For during the last week of Jesus' earthly ministry, they were quarrelling among themselves.
James and John wanted the chief places in the cabinet of the Kingdom.
They were jealous of each other.

They were not very brave.
When Jesus was arrested they all ran away.
After He died, they scattered and went underground.
They met behind closed doors.
No, they were not very brave.

They did not have much faith.
Thomas refused to believe that the Master had risen from
the dead until he had proof.
He even stipulated what that proof had to be.

Of course these three years did something to them and in
them.
The fuel had been laid on the fire, but it was not lit.
The seed had been sown, but it had not germinated.

All the possibilities of change in them had been created,
but the changes had not yet happened.
What did change them?
Not the crucifixion
   not the resurrection
      but the coming of the Holy Spirit at Pentecost.

Not until these men were filled with the Holy Ghost were
they changed.
Not until The Spirit had come upon them in power were
they changed,
   so that cowardice gave place to courage
      unbelief became a flaming faith and conviction that
      nothing on earth could shake
         jealousy was swallowed up in brotherly love
            self-interest was killed and became a ministry to
            others
               fear was banished, and they were afraid of no
               man . . . no threat, no danger.

And therein lies our hope.

We have not seen Jesus as they did.

We never heard the sound of His voice or saw the sunlight dance on His hair or traced His footprints in the sands of Palestine.

But we have the same opportunity to be changed, because the same Holy Spirit is available to us today.

He has been sent into the world to lead us into all truth.

to convict us of sin,

to be our Helper, our Guide.

This is a day of little faith—of few convictions—a day when men seem to have no great causes and no great passions.

So in frustration, in disappointment they are inclined to say "You can't change human nature".

It is true that we cannot change human nature.

But God can.

It is the modern heresy to think that human nature cannot be changed.

Human nature must be changed if we are ever to have an end to war,

or to correct the wrong situations that make our lives uneasy and our hearts sore.

Now Christianity, the power of Jesus Christ,

the Holy Spirit of God,

is the only force that can change people for good.

It is the only power in the world that can change the gears in a man's life from self-will to God's will.

It is the only power that can give a man the right motives— to do what God wants him to do.

Nothing else can bring him to seek first the Kingdom of God and His righteousness, and to want most of all *to be part of the answer to the world's ills, and not part of the problem*[2].

But how?

All that is needed is your own sincere desire,
   your willingness to confess your mistakes
      and your stubborn selfishness
and to face up to your sins.

When they are acknowledged and you begin to see yourself as God sees you,
and when you ask His forgiveness, the miracle has begun.

For forgiveness can be yours—now—right away—and you begin to be a new person from this moment.

When you yourself have begun to be a new person, then there is hope for your own problem whatever it is—hope for a solution to the strained relations in your office
hope for a better understanding and a discovery of a new love for your husband or wife, a new spirit in your home and a happiness you had thought was gone forever
hope for a new meaning to your life and a new reason for living
hope . . . hope . . . hope.
Don't give up.
There's still hope.

God hasn't given up yet on His world, which is one world, and could be one world of security, peace and brotherhood instead of two worlds of suspicion and fear.

God hasn't given up on this country, which is His latest experiment in human freedom and opportunity.

God hasn't given up on you.
He can still do great things for you, in you, and through you.
God is ready and waiting and able.
What about you, and me?

We are, after all, like lumps of clay.
There are brittle pieces, hard pieces.
We have little shape or beauty.
But we need not despair.
If we are clay, let us remember there is a Potter, and His wheel.

The old gospel song has it right:
　　"Have Thine own way, Lord,
　　Have Thine own way.
　　Thou art the Potter, I am the clay;
　　Mould me and make me, after Thy will,
　　While I am waiting, yielded and still".[3]

That's it.
We have only to be yielded, that is, willing, surrendered, and He will do the rest.
He will make us according to the pattern for which, in His love, He designed us.
And it will be good—for our own good—and for His glory.

Do not despair.
If you want to be different, you may.
You, too, can be changed for the better. Therein lies our hope—and the hope of the world.

We are disciples in clay.

And there is still the skill of the Potter.

Prayer

O Lord our God, even at this moment as we come blundering into Thy presence in prayer, we are haunted by memories of duties unperformed, promptings disobeyed, and beckonings ignored.

Opportunities to be kind knocked on the door of our hearts and went weeping away.

We are ashamed, O Lord, and tired of failure.

If Thou art drawing close to us now, come nearer still, till selfishness is burned out within us and our wills lose their weakness in union with Thine own. AMEN.

That which we call Salvation, and which is a most comprehensive term—is a free gift. You can't buy it, nor can you earn it. It is not a reward dangling before the Christian, like a carrot before a mule. It is not something that the Church has to peddle, and probably no idea hurts me more than suggesting that I am a salesman—endeavouring to sell people on the idea of religion. I resent it bitterly. I am not selling people anything. Religion is not for sale! It is a gift. It is given away.

From THE MANDATES OF JESUS

The Saint Of The Rank And File

IN ANY LIST of the apostles, most of us would begin by
   naming the triumvirate—
  Peter
    James
        and John, and then we go like this:
Peter . . . James . . . and John . . . and Matthew . . .
and Judas of course . . . and . . . and Philip . . . and,
oh, yes, Thomas . . .

let's see . . . and . . . and . . . who were the rest anyway?

Most of us know nothing much about Andrew—except
that he was Peter's brother, and one of the apostles.[4]

But we ought to know Andrew better than that, because
we see him every day.
He is the man who sits beside you on the bus.
He may be the fellow who blows the mailman's whistle
down the street . . .
or drives the street-car . . .
  or waits on you in the store . . .
or works at the next desk in your office . . .
  or sells you your ticket at the railroad station,
or even carries your bags.

Andrew is all around you.

You meet him every day, and he holds the key to many situations.
Andrew appears on the New Testament scene but seldom.
Perhaps we have not grasped all the significance of the appearances he does make.

But, first let us begin at the beginning.

Andrew's boyhood home was Bethsaida of Galilee.
It lay about seventy miles north of Jerusalem on the Sea of Galilee. It was there that Jesus found five of His twelve disciples—John and James, Philip, Peter and Andrew.

In Bethsaida we inquire for the house of Jonas, where live the two brothers Peter and Andrew, who with their father operate a fishing boat on the Sea of Galilee.
We find that Andrew is not at home, but they point out to us the house of Zebedee, where we may find him.

As we approach, we see two young men in earnest conversation with an old man who must be Zebedee, the father of James and John. The younger men are talking about a journey they hope to make down the Jordan to a ford, where they have heard a daring young preacher was drawing great crowds with a stirring message about the coming Kingdom of God.

The travellers are full of it.
The camel-drivers, as they swing north toward the ridges of Lebanon and on into Asia, can talk of nothing else, and these two young Galileans are anxious to see for themselves this striking young prophet.

"Yes, John", Zebedee is saying, "Andrew is just the com-

panion. You want to take him with you rather than Simon.
If Simon went along, he would do all the talking. He would
even do your thinking for you.

Why don't you two go by yourselves?
And if Simon should insist on going with you—you and
Andrew stay together. Make up your own minds.

And may the peace and blessing of God go with you".

We remember what happened when they arrived at the
place. They heard the message of John the Baptist—a
strange man who with piercing
   glowing eyes and eloquent tongue stirred
them as they had never been stirred before.

His prophecy and the fire in his eyes as he spoke won the
hearts of Andrew and John and they joined themselves to
John the Baptist.

In a very short time their attention was shifted from him to
Another, who, when He came, was announced by John as
"The Lamb of God which taketh away the sin of the world".

Later, they met Jesus and spent some time in personal
conversation with Him, and pledged themselves to become
His disciples. And the very first thing that Andrew did after
he found Jesus was to search out his own brother, Simon,
and introduce him to Christ.

Andrew went with Jesus when He came to Galilee and was
present when Jesus worked His first miracle.
Andrew saw Him at the marriage in Cana,
   saw Jesus with laughter in His eyes and smiles
tugging at the corners of His mouth.
Andrew was with Him in Judea when He baptized there.

Andrew probably was in the garden among the olive trees
when Nicodemus came to sit talking with Jesus about
spiritual things, until the dawn came up behind the hills.

Andrew had been with Jesus for a time as His public
ministry opened, and then apparently he went back to
Bethsaida.

Somehow, for Andrew, things did not seem the same.
He worked abstractedly;
   he day-dreamed a lot.
This was particularly exasperating to Peter and to their
partners,
   for Andrew seemed to be so preoccupied
     and clumsy
        and absent-minded.
They wondered if Andrew was in love.

Ah, maybe that was it!
Little did they know how true it was—for indeed he was in
love.
He had fallen completely in love with Jesus of Nazareth.
He was in love with a Voice.
  He was in love with a vision
    in love with a Face
      in love with a faith
and every day and every night he dreamed and wondered in
his heart about the things that Christ had said . . .
      "this kingdom of God on earth . . .".

The waves lapping against the boat seemed to be saying
over and over the things he had heard Him say.
   His voice was in the wind.
   His face was in the sunlight dancing on the waves.

So Andrew dreamed and waited.
Then came the never-to-be-forgotten day—that day of
the second call—
    when, as Simon and Andrew bent over their nets
spread across their knees, His shadow fell upon them and
they both looked up.

And Andrew's heart beat faster, for it was *He*—the Face,
the Voice . . .
Again He talked of that "Kingdom of God" . . .

He made a gesture with His hand—a beckoning sort of
gesture that brought them scrambling to their feet, and then
He said:
    "Come . . . come with me . . .
        and I will make you to become fishers of men".

They dropped their nets and their lines.
They turned their backs on the little village in which they
were born and went away, following Him Who spoke about
the Kingdom of God.

It was to be three years until they came back to their boats
again.
Thus Andrew became one of the twelve and was consecrated
as an apostle.

There is something significant in the fact that Andrew was
the first of the apostles to be called.
The choice was important, for it was the example of Andrew,
    the lead he gave
        and the influence he brought to bear upon the others
that to a large extent decided them.

Christ saw right away that the soul's unrest,
   the straining after higher things,
and the deeper knowledge of God which made Andrew
walk from Bethsaida to Bethany, indicated a promise of
large spiritual growth and a fertile field in which the seed
could be cast.

Andrew has usually been referred to as Simon Peter's
brother.
He himself was not a leader of men . . .
He was not aggressive like Simon.
We find him usually playing second fiddle to his famous
brother, and we know perfectly well that it takes a lot of
grace to play second fiddle.

It is not easy to live out your life day after day
      and week after week
  and year after year in a subordinate
position while somebody else gets the notice
          the publicity
        the attention
      the credit
     the praise
    the spotlight
and perhaps the reward.

It takes a lot of grace to accept a rôle like that, and yet
Andrew seems never to have complained.

Being the brother of Simon must have been hard all along.
We can imagine the children at play—it would be Simon
who would choose the sides . . .
    Simon who would nominate the game to be played . . .
    Simon who always spoke for them both . . .

And if they were walking along the road that wound round the head of the lake and some traveller inquired the way— it was always Simon who made reply, although Andrew knew it just as well as Simon.

In school, no doubt, they sat together, and again, no doubt, it would be Simon whose hand would go up in eagerness to give the answer.

Andrew had always had to play second fiddle, and yet he seemed to have done so with the best of grace.

When we look into the lives of these two brothers, it must be admitted that Andrew was not the great preacher Peter was.
He was not the great missionary leader who helped
    establish churches that were to spring up
  like flowers in the wilderness,
but it must never be forgotten *that it was Andrew who brought Peter to Christ.*

As Dr McKay has said,
"There would have been no eloquent Peter at Pentecost had there been no humble Andrew to bring him to Jesus".[5]

There are two pictures of Andrew in the New Testament that we might examine, for they show us the man better than any analysis we might make.

The first scene is late afternoon. The shadows of the sun have lengthened, and the long hot day is drawing to a close. The birds are winging their way homeward.
The crowd that has followed Jesus all day long, listening to His marvellous message, has forgotten time altogether.

But now they suddenly realize that soon night will fall, and they are hungry.
Children begin to whimper, tired and weary . . .
So Jesus asked His disciples how they could get enough bread to feed this crowd of people.

Then we read that it was Andrew who said:
"There is a boy here who has five barley loaves and a couple of fish, but what is that among so many people?"[6]

Now, have you ever wondered how Andrew knew about the lunch the boy was carrying?
I have, and I suggest to you that Andrew knew because he had made friends with the boy.
He had talked with him; perhaps the boy had been at his side all day.
Maybe the boy's mother had asked Andrew to keep an eye on him.

What would they talk about?
Well, Andrew was a fisherman.
There was much that would be of interest to the boy . . .
how to tie certain knots
how to fasten a fish hook on a line
all the tell-tales that indicate where the fish are
the part the weather plays in fishing.
There are many things that would be of interest to the boy.

I suppose it would be perfectly natural for the lad to share his lunch with Andrew—this man who had been so kind to him—so friendly.
But they decided that they would wait a bit and see what the Master intended to do.

At any rate, I believe Andrew was essentially interested in
people. I have heard it said many times, that a good index
to character is a man's ability to make friends
    with children
   and with dogs.
  I believe it to be true.
The man who can interest a boy and make friends with a
boy and who can win the confidence of a dog must be all
right.
Children and dogs, usually, are good judges of character
and of human nature.

The other glimpse we have of Andrew is when the Greeks
come and ask that they might see Jesus.
We read that they inquired of Philip, and he turned for
advice to Andrew, and it was Andrew who introduced
them to Jesus.

Have you ever wondered why Philip did not go himself?
I suggest to you that Andrew had by this time a knack of
introducing people to Jesus, and had done it so often that
they all turned to him.

Andrew first comes to our attention introducing his own
brother Simon to the Lord.
Here now, he is introducing Greeks.
He really might be called Andrew the Introducer.
Andrew is not one of the greatest of the disciples, but he is
typical of those men of broad sympathy and sound common
sense, without whom the success of any great movement
cannot be assured.

It is all very well to be impressed with the contributions to
human happiness that are made by the world's leaders—the

E

great men and women—the five-talent people
    who do things
  do them well
and who usually get the notice
      the publicity
    the praise
and the rewards.

But what we are all inclined to forget is the fact that behind
them are unnumbered hosts of ordinary men and women
whose names are never printed
    whose faces are never captured by the newsreel cameras
      but whose quiet unassuming labour makes the work
      of the leaders possible.

The vast majority of people fall into the two-talent class—
the useful hosts of mediocrity
    the average men and women
      who are always taken for granted
        but without whom nothing could ever be accom-
        plished.
They are willing to play second fiddle.
They know that they will not be singled out for honours or
medals.

They have a job to do, and they are willing to do it without
complaint,
and often with bravery and consecration of the highest
order.

They are willing—not only to lose their identities in the
job to be done, but even to lose their lives for the sake of
others.

64

They have discovered the truth of the paradox of Christianity
that only by losing one's life can one find it.

The Battle of Britain, in the last war, which lasted from
August 8 to October 31, 1940, cost the Germans 2,375
planes
    destroyed in daylight alone,
  and many more at night.
It cost the British 375 pilots killed and 358 wounded.

A handful of RAF fliers had saved Britain,
  and perhaps the world
    from destruction.
You will remember what Winston Churchill said of his
people:
  "Never in the field of human conflict was so much owed
  by so many to so few!"
That victory was achieved, you see,
  not by the top-ranking generals
    the brass hats
      the big shots
but by young men—a team—playing and fighting—and
dying together.

Another example was afforded in the famous retreat to
Dunkirk after the collapse of the Maginot Line and the
surrender of Belgium.
Covering the retreat was the 51st Division of the British
Army, Scottish troops of regiments with famous names.
They stood at St. Valerie to make the evacuation possible.

They were a road block, whose only job was to hold back
the Panzer divisions long enough to permit the motley
fleet of small boats, manned by the nameless volunteers, to

take off as many British and French soldiers as they could.

Well, the 51st did their job well. They were lost . . . expendable . . .
 but they did their job and made Dunkirk possible.

To fellow members of St. Andrew's Societies across this country I would say this: "Remember the name you bear." If we are St. Andrew's men, we must exemplify the characteristics of our patron saint.

How could I sum them up?
 A self-effacing ministry to those in need.
A willingness to play second fiddle, if need be,
 in order that the job can be done.

There are times when this is hard for the Scot,
 for he is not only independent
he has a strong confidence in his own ability.
This is often mistaken for conceit and boastfulness.
It does not grow out of his egotism at all,
 for the Scot is traditionally a modest man—reticent and shy.
He does not wear his heart on his sleeve.

He is an enigma to the Englishman—
 for whereas the Sassenach is emotional at times
 the Scot is phlegmatic.
But beware of the strong currents that run deep in the Scottish heart.

General Montgomery has said that in the Eighth Army the troops most easily raised to a high pitch of enthusiasm and

high morale for the fight were the troops of the Highland
Division.

These are the traits of character most sorely needed in our
world today—a willingness to play second fiddle
   or, if you prefer,
      humility,
and that broad sympathy and sound common-sense, without
which the success of any great movement cannot be
measured.

You see, it is the Andrews that are the glory of any democracy . . . the people who do the mundane things of our
work-a-day life.
For example, think of the garbage collectors.
Do you realize how important they are?
Theirs is not a pleasant job, but there are few jobs more
important to the health and well-being of all of us.

You see, it is the Andrews after all who carry on the work
of the nation and of the church.
For after all the five-talent men and women have flashed
like meteors through the skies
   leaving behind a trail of glory
after their great gifts for organization
after all their visions and their plans
   they depend upon Andrew to do the job.

So, the success of the whole business largely depends upon
Andrew,
for Andrew was interested in people
   and Andrew brought them to Christ.
Only as the church today is interested in people and will
bring them to Christ can the work go forward.

The work that needs to be done today is the work that Andrew is best able to do.

It is the work of the ordinary men and women in the church, and Andrew is their patron saint.

It is not without significance that Andrew was chosen to be the Patron Saint of Scotland, and St. Andrew's cross, a diagonal white cross on a blue ground, is the foundation on which St. George's cross of England and St. Patrick's cross of Ireland were laid to make the Union Jack.

Andrew was at the bottom.

It is always so—in everything that is worth while—
    everything that is good and true.

It is supported by Andrew—the two-talent man.

Each time Andrew appears on the New Testament scene he is introducing someone to Jesus.

"Only two talents?"

Aye, but the two talents are surrendered to Christ.

Andrew, we too would meet the Master!

Prayer

Lord Jesus, bless all who serve us, who have dedicated their lives to the ministry of others—all the teachers of our schools who labour so patiently with so little appreciation; all who wait upon the public, the clerks in the stores who have to accept criticism, complaints, bad manners, selfishness at the hands of a thoughtless public. Bless the mailman, the drivers of streetcars and buses who must listen to people who lose their tempers.

Bless every humble soul who, in these days of stress and strain, preaches sermons without words. AMEN.

Prayer, like everything else in God's universe, is not accidental in its way of working.

It is based on laws—spiritual laws—in their field just as constant and inexorable and fixed as their companions in the natural realm.

From THE LOST SECRET

Research Unlimited

DURING THE LIFETIME of most of us, science and invention has made its greatest strides.

Everybody over forty can remember the mood of optimism that marked the first decade of the twentieth century.

People then were living in the days of the first telephones perfected for general use
the first express trains
the first uses of electricity
the first internal combustion engine.
Great things were in prospect.

Since most of us were born, the automobile has been developed, until there is now one car for about every five persons in America. Electric lighting and electricity for many home uses are commonplace.

The radio and television, which can bring into your living room or bedroom, music
drama
advertising
and the latest news
are now taken for granted.

The aeroplane no longer amazes, but whisks us across the continent from breakfast to supper.

71

Motion pictures have become a weekly diet.
Electric eyes open doors at our approach, and radar enables
us to see in the dark.
Penicillin and sulfa drugs have conquered many a germ, and
atomic energy has opened a vast new world.

All of this since most of us were born . . .

These latest inventions and discoveries have made war more
terrible, and while they have given us many conveniences
and comforts, they have made life more complicated
    peace more difficult
        and the human heart more troubled.

Undoubtedly we have improved means—
    but unfortunately, we have not improved ends.
We have better ways of getting there,
    but we have no better places to go.
We can save more time, but we are not making any better
use of the time we save.

Everyone agrees that we have made far more advances in
the scientific world than we have made in the world of
morals and ethics.
Spiritually, we have not kept pace with our progress in the
realm of science and invention.

If great advances *have* been made in the realm of the spirit,
then either they have not been reported or publicized,
    or we have chosen to ignore them . . .
else we are forced to the conclusion that they have not been
made at all.

We hang on every word reporting the doings of the

atomic scientists.
We are aware of them and their work.

We shudder to recall the fruits of their labours that we
know, and we can only cross our fingers as we hope that
good and not unbelievable horror will result from their
discoveries.

We lap up every word describing new inventions, and we
eagerly discuss and examine pictures of new weapons
    new automobiles
  and new gadgets.
Why is it that we have so little interest in spiritual discoveries
  —new discoveries of God
    of God's working in His world
      of God's dealing with His people?

Why is it that we are so little curious about the discovery
of new techniques for living and new ideas that would make
for our happiness and the peace of the world?

The scientists have forged far ahead.
What they have invented and provided for us has out-
stripped our moral character
  our spiritual quality
    and our religious faith.
Scientific discovery has gone far ahead of man's progress
in the moral realm.
That is the trouble.

Some people have thought that the more science we have,
the more religion can be discarded.
But that is not so.

Rather, the fact is that the more science we have, the more we need character-building religion.

The more we know about science, the more we realize that there is a point in life at which science has to stop—but we have to go on.

All the high hopes built on scientific gifts and invention have crashed to the ground, as we have been forced to face the realistic fact that man can be so insane and so corrupt that the more power you give him, the more widely will he destroy himself.

That is why the atomic scientists, those brilliant men who delved into the secrets of nuclear energy, are so troubled and conscience-stricken.

The human conscience, which has been anaesthetized by the mechanical progress of the last fifty years, has been awakened.

We are now at the place where we see that progress simply must be made in the realm of morals and ethics and character, if civilization is to be saved.

The time has come when we must face the solving of the world's true problems—the human problems . . .

The problem of lying—which is called propaganda . . .
  the problem of selfishness—which is called nationalism or self-interest . . .
    the problem of greed—which is often called profit or good business . . .
      the problem of licence disguised as liberty . . .
    the problem of lust masquerading as love . . .

74

the challenge of materialism—the hook that is baited with security . . .

These are the problems that confront us now.

Science has its foundation in research.
Its discoveries all rest upon the patience
    willingness
  and open-minded seeking
of thousands of men and women who have taken one single proposition and sat down humbly before it to explore and to test it a great number of times
    under varying conditions
  and then to report the results.

Suppose that in this same way there were a comparable number of young men and women setting out to get their Master's degree, or to write their Ph.D. thesis on their findings, after months of careful experiment with such propositions as these:
    "Therefore take no thought, saying What shall we eat? or, What shall we drink? or Wherewithal shall we be clothed? . . . for your heavenly Father knoweth that ye have need of all these things.

    "But seek ye first the kingdom of God and his righteousness and all these things shall be added unto you" (MATTHEW 6 : 31-33).

Or this one . . .

    "Ask, and it shall be given you; seek, and ye shall find; knock and it shall be opened unto you" (MATTHEW 7 : 7).

Or . . .

> "Therefore I say unto you, What things soever ye desire, when ye pray, believe that ye receive them, and ye shall have them" (MARK 11 : 24).

Or this one . . .

> "If any of you lack wisdom, let him ask of God, that giveth to all men liberally, and upbraideth not; and it shall be given him" (JAMES 1 : 5).

Or, take the text, with God's challenge to research:

> ". . . prove me now herewith, saith the Lord of hosts, if I will not open you the windows of heaven, and pour you out a blessing, that there shall not be room enough to receive it".

This sort of research could advance much faster than physical science, which requires special laboratories
 perfect conditions
and expensive equipment.
For it's the sort of research that anyone can pursue.

You say you have no time?
Any one of us could delve into it where we are
 as we are
 in our present jobs,
and it would make our jobs new and exciting, humdrum no longer.

No time?
Did you ever stop to think that most of the world's great

men have achieved their true life work, not in the course of their needful occupations, but *in their spare time.*

A tired-out rail splitter, crouched over his tattered books by candlelight at the day's end,
  preparing for his future, instead of snoring or sky-larking like his co-labourers—
Lincoln cut out his path to later immortality *in his spare time.*

An underpaid and overworked telegraph clerk stole hours from sleep, or from play, at night, trying to crystallize into realities certain fantastic dreams in which he had faith.
Today, the whole world is benefiting by what Edison did—
in his spare time.

An instructor in an obscure college varied the drudgery he hated, by spending his evenings and holidays in tinkering with a queer device of his at which his fellow teachers laughed.
But he invented the telephone—*in his spare time.*

You, too, have spare time.
Why not use it in this kind of research which pays wonderful dividends in this life and the next?

Suppose, for example, that a group of Christians decided to experiment with the Lord's exhortation to tithe for one year. What do you suppose the results would be?

The tithe is the form of giving advocated in the Bible.
All through the Old Testament, the principle of dedicating the tenth to God is taught and observed.
So much was it a part of the habits and customs of men of

that day that in New Testament times it was taken for granted—
   something that simply was expected of men of integrity.

Jesus expected it of men of God.
He felt it was only when a man began to give above his tenth that he was showing real generosity.

"Bring ye all the tithes into the storehouse, that there may be meat in mine house, and prove me now herewith, saith the Lord of hosts, if I will not open you the windows of heaven, and pour you out a blessing, that there shall not be room enough to receive it".

What if we were challenged to try it out for a year?

It would seem from history that God often gives individual believers a specific emphasis on some phase of the Christian Gospel.

He lays upon the heart of one person—
   like William Plumber Jacobs, who founded Thornwell Orphanage in Clinton, South Carolina . . .
   or Brother Bryan, of beloved memory, in Birmingham, Alabama, who ran his church, who fed and clothed the poor of the neighbourhood . . .
   or George Müller, who maintained an orphanage, in Bristol, England . . .
to test to the limit His promise to provide material needs.

"Seek ye first the kingdom of God and his righteousness, and all these things shall be added unto you".
These men believed it.
They decided to try it out.

Müller became so convinced of God's trustworthiness in practical affairs that he closed one door after another behind him in order to prove it to the world.

First, he refused to accept a regular salary for his preaching. Next, he literally sold all that he had and gave to the poor. His wife concurred in this decision, and they parted with all their household furnishings.

When he felt led to open one of the first orphanages in England, he did so and conducted it always under these principles:
He never told anyone of the financial needs of the orphanage except God.
   He forbade his helpers to tell outsiders of their needs.
      He never borrowed.
         He never used money for one thing that had been given for another.

Many times the supply of food in the orphanage was on a day-to-day basis, and sometimes it was meal-to-meal,
   but there was always something to eat.
You can read in Müller's own journal where he prayed the night before for the next day's needs . . .
   and you can turn the page and see how in the morning, the need was supplied—often in a most surprising way.

Roland Brown, or "Pastor Brown" as he is widely known, is another who kept books on the Lord's daily dealings with him and his church.
A Chicago Baptist minister, he was greatly troubled by the physical needs of his congregation.
He saw cancer eating away in the body of more than one of his beloved parishioners . . .

F

heart trouble
neuroses of various types
nervous breakdowns
all things that neither he nor their doctors could help.

Deeply troubled, as he pored over the promises of God in the Bible, he prayed many years that God would enable him to meet those needs.

Suddenly his prayers for the sick began to be answered. To give God all the credit, and to make such glorious findings available to the world, he kept a card file in strict scientific form.

These case histories have been and may be examined by any inquirer:
"Name of patient
disease or disorder
duration of illness
name of attending physician
name of hospital, if patient were hospitalized
the exact method of prayer
the date the prayer was made
the date on which healing was completed
doctor's diagnosis after healing".
It is all down in black and white.

What a vast field for research lies here.

If you are a sceptic, as most people today are in this field— would it not be worth your while to investigate in those cases where doctors can do nothing?

For you see, there are still miracles being performed.

80

I have seen them happen.
Still, in these latter days, there are clear evidences of God's
power working in human affairs.
That we must admit.

God has not withdrawn any power that was available in the
days of the first disciples.
There is certainly no indication in the Bible that the power
given to them was for a certain period only,
    or to work in a certain location.

It was not like a free trial offer advertised "good only for
thirty days".
If the other elements in the Gospel message were to have
universal application,
    and to hold true until Christ returned,
why not this element of healing,
that has always had such a strong appeal to human hearts
and is so wistfully remembered by those in trouble?

There is nothing in the Gospels to give the slightest hint
that Christ ever thought that sickness would in any way
help man's spiritual life,
    or that the Kingdom of God would be better furthered by
    bad health rather than by good health.

I could not believe,
nor can you, I am sure, that Christ would ever have
looked upon someone suffering from arthritis
        or cancer
    or leprosy, and have said:
"My friend, I am sorry for you.
But you must be brave.

God has sent this upon you for some good reason.
Don't ask me to heal you".

Why, Christ's view of God was just the opposite of that.
He would have violently denied such a caricature of His
Father.

Everywhere He went, Christ was confronted with sickness
and disease,
    and everywhere He did something about it.
Yet, there were times when He could do no mighty works,
as Mark puts it, because of unbelief.
Where there was no faith, He was powerless.
And there were many cases of sickness where no healing
was sought.

"But", someone will say, "that was all very well for Christ
to do these things,
    for, after all, He was the Son of God.
He had powers unique as He Himself was unique".

True—but He promised the same powers to His disciples.
Christ said:
    "Verily, verily, I say unto you,
    he that believeth on me, the works that I do shall he do
    also, and greater works than these shall he do, because I
    go unto my Father".

Now, for some reason or other, we are inclined to skip over
that promise,
    or to spiritualize it
as though by the passing of the centuries the words have
lost the meaning they apparently had to the first disciples.

The truth is that the Church has permitted this breath-taking part of the Gospel to fall out of it.
Is the "good news" only for the soul?
Is it simply for the life to come, with no application to the life that now is?

I believe it is there—in the good news He brought.
I believe it is one of the church's lost secrets that we must find again if we are to proclaim a full gospel
as "the most powerful form of energy that one can generate".

But why are there so few spiritual discoveries to match the progress made by science?

The answer lies in a lack of researchers.

Men have been willing to let mosquitoes bite them in the interests of science and human welfare.
How many are willing to give themselves away to take risks in spiritual research?

No one yet has ever set out to test God's promises fairly, thoroughly, and humbly, and had to report that God's promises don't work.
On the contrary, given a fair opportunity, God always surprises and overwhelms those who truly seek, with His bounty and His power.

Both scientific and spiritual advances have come about as a result of great need goading men to try anything, until they find something that works.

Science has now developed so far as to branch out in

providing many things we don't really need.
Spiritually, however, we are still in the area of dire necessity
to keep our very souls alive, lest they die of malnutrition.

We cannot do much for the world, until, first of all, we
have done something with ourselves.
The longer an orchestra plays, the more it needs to be tuned
up.
The further an aeroplane flies, the more it requires ground
service to put it into shape again.
There is no evading that law in any realm.

But here we are. We have money,
        We are well-clothed . . .
      We are comfortably housed . . .
    We have automobiles . . .
  and all the latest gadgets in our homes.
But *we are spiritually undernourished*.

We have neglected spiritual food.
Without spiritual exercise, our souls are soft and flabby.
The temptation is powerful to become so obsessed with the
urgent, brutal facts of the immediate world that faith in
Christ and His way of living becomes like a lovely im-
practical dream
    a pious hope
      a frail illusion.

But remember how that lovely dream started in the first
place—
    in a world mastered by military empire,
      and filled with the thundering tramp of Caesar's
      legions—
    in a little occupied country—

84

a dream shared by a handful of simple folk, ordinary men and women.

This little group, believing in a spiritual message, accepted the tension of living in two violently antagonistic worlds—Rome's and Christ's—
   and it was they who, in the end, survived.

The challenge today, pointed and heated by the atomic bomb, is still what it always was—
   a challenge to spiritual research.

Prayer

Lord Jesus, we come to Thee now as little children. Dress us again in clean pinafores; make us tidy once more with the tidiness of true remorse and confession. Oh, wash our hearts, that they may be clean again. Make us to know the strengthening joys of the Spirit, and the newness of life which only Thou can give.
AMEN.

There is no disgrace in being homesick. At times, I have felt the tugging of those invisible fingers and heard the whispering of those voices . . .

For I have seen the hills of Scotland moist with mist . . . have seen the fir trees marching down to the loch-sides; have seen the sheep on the hills and the heather in bloom; have heard the skirling of the pipes down the glen and the gurgling of the burn over the rocks . . . and the familiar music of the kettle on the hob; have seen pictures that will never fade, and sounds that will never die away.

I have longed for the northland . . . to see again the low stone houses, the swelling hills, the white tails of the waterfalls.

I have wanted to hear again the gentle low voices of the women and the music of the Gaelic tongue . . . "Guid save us a' . . ."; to smell the delicate fragrance of bluebells in the spring and the rhododendron; to hear the mavis sing . . . and the lark.

I have wanted to see the long twilights, to look out over the waters of the Firth, and be grateful to God that there was still more of Scotland beyond . . .

From PARDON THE SCOTTISH ACCENT

The Rock That Moved

THERE ARE NOT many cities in the heart of which you may suddenly hear the crowing of a cock.

That is one sound that is not likely to arouse the guests in any of Washington's downtown hotels.

One will never hear it in Times Square
       at Broad and Market
     at Five Points
   at Woodward and Michigan
 or along Michigan Boulevard.
Yet even to this day you may hear it in Jerusalem, for Jerusalem is different.

One who was visiting the Holy City was enjoying the quiet of his room when suddenly the silence was pierced by the shrill crowing of a cock, and he immediately thought of a man named Peter, for whom the trumpet of the dawn opened the floodgates of memory.

What would it do for some lonely, homesick young woman in Washington if, before the city has yawned itself into action, she were to hear the familiar bugle of the farmyard?

In a tide of sudden nostalgia she would be back home again
   on the plains of Kansas
      in the mountains of western North Carolina

among the red barns of a farm in Ohio
on the rolling green countryside of Pennsylvania
or among the red clay hills of Georgia.

There is many a young man in the city, bright in the night-time like day, his pulses racing with the throb of jungle drums and the moan of the saxophone, intoxicated with the lure of the city and in strong temptation, who could be saved were he to hear once again on the heavy night air the lowing of homeward-driven cattle and the calls of the old farmyards.

It is in mysterious and different ways that God comes to the rescue. He has a hundred ways of plucking at a man's sleeve.
He nudges some.
Others He taps on the shoulder.
To some it comes in music, to some in a picture, a story or a chance meeting on the street.
All these are used by God, who keeps watch over His own.

One St. Andrew's Day—a date all Scotsmen remember, I attended the annual banquet and had an emotional experience I shall not soon forget.

The Irish flaunt the shamrock in March, and the English remember Saint George and the dragon in June.
But to the Scot the 30th of November is one time when he throws aside his accustomed modesty and forgets he has always been outnumbered by the English eight to one, for this night is his own.
It is the night of the tartan and the haggis
the night for thoughts of home . . . a night for memories.

The hotel was filled with bagpipe music.
The skirl of the pipes, indescribably thrilling to the Scot,
came dancing into every conversation, and must have made
them wonder who had no Scottish blood.
There was a full pipe band—and a good one it was.
There were the old Scottish songs, and the Doric—the
broad Scots tongue, soft and kindly and warm.
There were the kilts and the glengarries, the Balmorals and
the honest faces of the sons of the land of the mountain and
the mist.

My, what memories came back, as the drumsticks twirled
above the drum, and the kettledrums rolled . . .
and our feet tapped out the time to Cock o' the North
      The Forty-Second
    and Hieland Laddie.

In memory I saw a battalion of the Gordon Highlanders,
swinging down from Edinburgh Castle on to Princes Street
when I was last in Scotland—the pipes skirling
    and the kilts swinging
with the pride that only Scotsmen fully know.

I thought of the Fifty-first Division at El Alamein going
through the German mine-fields to the blood-tingling call
of the bagpipes.

I thought of home . . . and long ago . . . and choked
back many a lump in my throat.
We sang the old songs . . . the songs my mither sang . . .
and many an eye was misty.
We didn't say very much. Words were useless.
We just averted our eyes and blinked a bit and swallowed
hard.

Memories . . . they come surging back into the heart to make it clean again . . . or to accuse it.

Yes . . . to some it is music . . . or a song.
   To others it is a picture or the face of a friend
but to Simon Peter it was the crowing of a cock.

He had seen the last flickering torch disappear round the turn of the path that wound down hill.
Only once in a while could the lights of the procession be seen through the trees—like giant fireflies.

The murmur of voices died away.
      the crackling of twigs
   and the rustling of dislodged stones through the grass.
There swept over Peter the realization that his Master had at last been captured and was marching away to die.

The icy fear that gripped his heart was a startling contrast to the flaming courage with which he drew his short sword a few minutes before, for this was a different Peter.

He realized that he had blundered, and that he had been rebuked.
Disappointed and puzzled, he could not understand the calm submission with which Christ permitted them to bind His hands and march Him off, as a butcher would lead an animal to the slaughter.

Realizing that he stood alone in the deserted garden, Peter stumbled blindly down the trail, heedless of the twigs that lashed his face and tore at his robes.

Stumbling on down-hill, instinctively hurrying to catch up

with the others, and yet not anxious to get too close, he followed down to the foot of the Mount of Olives, across the brook Kedron, and back up the hill to old Jerusalem, still asleep and quiet.

The procession made first for the house of Annas, into which they escorted Jesus. The heavy door creaked shut behind Him, and when Peter approached timidly, it was to find John standing there.

John persuaded the girl stationed at the door to let them in, and as they slipped past her, she scrutinized Peter and said to him:
  "Art not thou also one of this man's disciples?"
He said: "I am not".

Perhaps she felt that she could speak to Peter.
Perhaps she felt sorry for him, seeing the hurt, wounded look in his eyes and the pain in his face.

Who knows what was in her mind?
Perhaps she had seen the Master as they led Him in, and felt the irresistible attraction of the Great Galilean.

Perhaps in that brief moment, as they had crowded past her, *He had looked at her.*
If He had—then something may have happened to her, within her own heart.
Her faith might have been born,
a fire kindled by the spark the winds of strange circumstance had blown from the altar fires in the heart of the Son of God.

Perhaps she wanted to ask Peter more about the Master.
Perhaps she would have said—had Peter acknowledged Him:

91

"Tell me the sound of His voice.
   Is it low and sweet, vibrant?
Tell me of some of His miracles.
   Tell me how you are sure He is the Messiah.
What is this salvation He speaks about?
   How can we live forever?"

Maybe these questions would have come tumbling in a torrent from her lips . . . who knows?

But whatever she meant, whatever her motive for asking the question, "Art not thou also one of this man's disciples?" Peter denied his Lord and said: "I am not".

We can only stand aghast at Peter and wonder if the strain and the shock have destroyed his memory.

Simon, surely you remember the first day you saw Him?
Andrew and yourself floating the folded net . . . His shadow falling across you as you worked.
Don't you remember His command, His beckoning finger, the light in His eyes as He said: "Follow me, and *I will make you fishers of men*"?[7]

Peter, don't you remember?
And that night when Nicodemus came into the garden looking for the Master, don't you remember how he crept in with his cloak pulled up over his face?

Don't you remember how he frightened you, and how the Lord and Nicodemus talked for hours about the promises?
Don't you remember the wedding in Cana where He turned the water into wine?
Do you remember the music of His laugh

and the Samaritan woman at Sychar?
Don't you remember these things, Simon?

And now, they brought the Lord from Annas to Caiaphas,
and the soldiers and the temple guards mingled with the
servants in the courtyard.

Because the night was cold, they had kindled a fire in the
brazier, and Peter joined himself to the group, and stretching
out his hands warmed himself at their fire.

Peter was glad to join the hangers-on huddled round the
blaze, for the morning air bit sharply,
    and he found himself shivering. . . .
It was a kindly glow of warmth.

Coarse laughter greeted every joke and they discussed the
things such people talk about:
    the coming cock-fight in Jerusalem
        the new dancing girl in the court of Herod
            the prowess of the garrison's drivers
                the gambling losses of their friends
                    the latest news from Rome.

Peter was not paying much attention to their conversation
until one of the soldiers nudged him and said:
    "Thou art also of them".
And Peter said, for the second time: "Man, *I am not*".

Peter, you must remember . . . surely . . . it must be
that you are afraid.
Your brave heart must have turned to water.
Surely you cannot have forgotten . . .

many a time . . . crossing the lake in a boat like your own,
   with its worn seats
      its patched sails, slanting in the sun
         and its high rudder?

Remember the night He came walking on the water, and
you tried it, and were walking, like the Master, until your
courage left you . . . your faith gave way?

Simon, has your courage left you again?

Have your forgotten the pool at Bethesda and how you
laughed when the impotent man rose up . . .
      rolled up his bed
    threw it over his shoulder
  and went away leaping in the air and shouting?

Ah, Simon, you spoke so bravely . . . and now here you
are.

For the next hour or so they merely waited.
What was keeping them so long? They little knew the
difficulty of getting witnesses to agree.
They little knew that sleepless men, with tempers raw and
irritated, were trying to find some reason that they could
submit to Pilate that would justify their demands for the
death of Jesus.

After an hour had passed, there joined the group a soldier
who had come out of the palace.
As he greeted his friends in the circle, his eye fell on Peter.
He scrutinized him very carefully, and Peter, feeling the
examination of the newcomer, looked round as the soldier
asked: "Did not I see thee in the garden with Him?"

One of his friends joined in:
  "Certainly—he's one of the Galileans.
  Just listen to his accent".
And the soldier stubbornly went on: "I am sure I saw him in
the garden, for my kinsman, Malchus, was wounded by one
of them—who drew a sword,
and if I am not mistaken—it was this fellow here".

Then Peter, beginning to curse and to swear, said:
  "I know not the man".

He used language he had not used for years.
It was vile. . . . Even the soldiers were shocked.
They all looked at him in amazement.

They did not appear to notice the shuffling of feet, as
soldiers led Christ from Caiaphas to Pilate.
Perhaps they did not make much noise. They were tired
    worn with argument and talk
  so they were very quiet.

The group standing round the fire was silent, shocked at the
vehemence and the profanity of Peter's denial.
It was a torrent of foulness, but it was his face that startled
them. It was livid
    distorted
  eyes blazing
  mouth snarling like a cornered animal.
It was not a pleasant sight, and they kept silent.
It was a silence so intense that the crowing of a distant
cock was like a bugle call . . .

Immediately, Peter remembered the Lord's prophecy:
  "Before the cock crow twice, thou shalt deny me thrice".

G

Like a wave there swept over him the realization of what he had done. All of a sudden he remembered what Jesus had said, and with tears streaming down his face, he turned away from the fire.

Through a mist of tears he saw ahead of him the stairway that led to Pilate's palace . . .
and by a terrible Providence, it was just at that moment that Christ was being led up the stairs to appear before Pilate.

The Lord had heard!
   The Lord had heard every hot searing word . . .
      The Lord had heard the blistering denial . . .
         the foul, fisherman's oaths . . .
He—He had heard it all!

Christ paused on the stair, and looked down over the rail—
looked right into the very soul of Peter.
The eyes of the two met . . . at that awful moment.

Through his tears all else was a blur to Peter,
but that one face shone through the tears . . .
   that lovely face
      that terrible face
         those eyes—sad
            reproachful
               tender . . . as if they understood and forgave.
Ah, how well he knew Him, and how much he loved Him.

The world seemed to stand still, as for that terrible moment,
Peter looked at the One he denied.
We shall never know what passed between them.
Christ seemed to say again:
   "But I have prayed for thee, Simon.

96

Satan hath desired to have thee.
But I have prayed for thee".

His tears now overflowed and ran down his cheeks—
 hot and scalding tears they were—
and with great sobs shaking his strong frame, Peter spun
round and rushed out to have the cool morning air fan his
burning cheeks.

He fled with his heart pounding in his breast, while the
Nazarene walked steadily to meet the Roman governor.

Something died within the heart of Peter that night.
Something was killed. That's why his heart was broken.

In fact, *the Simon in him was killed*
 the old arrogant boasting bravado of Simon
  the cocksure confidence of the strong fisherman
   the impetuous stubbornness
    the impulsive thoughtlessness of Simon . . .
these all died in that moment.

Simon had ceased to be. Peter was being born.

Nothing more is heard of Peter for two days.
Christ has been crucified.

The hammer blows seem to be re-echoing still among the
temple domes, and in the very heart of Peter he feels the
thud of the hammer and hears the screaming of the impeni-
tent thief.

But we must follow Peter further. It is not fair to leave him a
sinner, a swearing traitor, a fugitive from the heart of love.

This apprentice apostle is still in the making.
And he is running true to form.

Only last night the Master had spoken a personal word of
warning when He said:
"Simon, Simon, behold Satan hath desired to have thee
that he may sift you as wheat—"
and it had come true.

But he remembered that word of hope added by Jesus:
"But I have prayed for thee that thy faith fail not".

His Lord had prayed that somehow he should not fail.
That prayer must be—would be answered—but how?
Never again would his Master trust him.

And what of the other disciples? What would they think of
him? What could he do?

Ah, but Jesus had said even more:
"And when thou art converted"—that is, turned around
—when you have got new bearings
when you turn your face once more toward me—
"strengthen thy brethren".
What did He mean?
"Black Saturday passed.
A new day dawned . . . a new week . . .
aye, indeed, a new age . . . though they knew it not".[8]

There came the strange story gasped out by breathless
women who had come running from the tomb.
Then a race with John and the discovery of the empty
grave . . .

98

Then the strange tale of the two disciples who came back from Emmaus.

Something had happened.
Life could never be the same again.
The dead had come to life.

The Christ who had been crucified was alive, but still Simon could only nurse his deep and bitter shame.
He was a changed man, still smarting with the searing of the iron that had eaten into his very soul.

There came that night when, having gone back to their boats and their nets, they had worked hard and in comparative silence. Now as they came back, discouraged and sad, they saw Someone standing on the beach in the early light of morning. The sea was calm—calm as a millpond—and the light, early morning mist still clung to the surface of the water.
They saw the flames leaping from a fire, and this mysterious figure waiting while their boat drew nearer to the shore.

"It is the Lord", said John, and that was enough for Simon. Here was the opportunity for which he had longed—to tell the Lord that he loved Him—to show how well he knew Him.

Without a moment's hesitation, he jumped overboard and waded ashore.
And then comes the loveliest record of God dealing with a penitent sinner . . .
Its tenderness and understanding come stealing into our own hearts like the perfume of crushed flowers.

For every denial Jesus asked a pledge of love.
Three times the question: "Simon, . . . lovest thou me?"
Three times the answer—and then the restoration,
"Feed my lambs. . . . Feed my sheep. . . . Feed my sheep".
"And when he had spoken this, he saith unto him, Follow me".
When next we see Simon, he is Simon no more—
but Peter—the Rock.

We see him fearless and eloquent
fire in his eyes
and his voice vibrant with conviction
melodious with good news.
His own will has gone; his Master's will has taken its place.
Peter stands up and preaches the gospel of his crucified and risen Lord.

Is this Simon preaching a sermon?
No, this is Peter.

Simon which was—the rock which had moved, but now is firmly established in the gospel.
The sinner-saint has become a witness
a pillar of strength to the brethren
an apostle to the ages.

The same Jesus who called Simon is calling you.
The same Jesus who saved Simon can save you.
The same mighty hand will hold you up.

The denials that you have made were made by Simon.
Yet he was restored; so may you be restored.

Christ changed Simon into Peter,
the sinner into the saint.

He can change your life, if you are willing!

Prayer

May our prayer, O Christ, awaken all Thy human reminiscences, that we may feel in our hearts the sympathizing Jesus. Thou hast walked this earthly vale and hast not forgotten what it is to be tired, what it is to know aching muscles, as Thou didst work long hours at the carpenter's bench. Thou hast not forgotten what it is to feel the sharp stabs of pain, or hunger or thirst. Thou knowest what it is to be forgotten, to be lonely. Thou dost remember the feel of hot and scalding tears running down Thy cheeks.

O, we thank Thee that Thou wert willing to come to earth and share with us the weaknesses of the flesh, for now we know that Thou dost understand all that we are ever called upon to bear. We know that Thou, Our God, art still able to do more than we ask or expect. So bless us, each one, not according to our deserving, but according to the riches in glory of Christ Jesus, our Lord. AMEN.

Christ has suffered for our sins. He has paid the penalty for us, so that there is therefore no condemnation to them that are in Christ Jesus. He has, with His own blood, written "Paid" across the ledgers of Heaven.

From THE HISTORIC JESUS: FACTS OR FANCIES

Were You There?

THE MORNING SUN, with probing rays, had roused the City of David. Already pilgrims and visitors were pouring in through the gates, mingling with merchants from the villages round about;
shepherds coming in from the hills,
and the narrow streets were crowded.

There were the aged, stooped with years, muttering to themselves as they pushed through the throngs.
There were children playing in the streets,
calling to each other in shrill voices.

There were men and women carrying burdens
baskets of vegetables
casks of wine
and water bags.
Tradesmen with their tools seemed out of place in the holiday atmosphere.

Here a donkey stood sleepily beneath his burden in the sunlight.
There under a narrow canopy a merchant shouted his wares in a pavement stall.
It was not easy to make one's way through the crowd.

It was especially difficult for the procession that started out from the governor's palace.

At its head rode a Roman centurion, disdainful and aloof,
scornful alike of child or cripple who might be in his way.

His lips curled in thin lines of contempt as he watched
through half-shut eyes the shouting, jeering crowd.

Before him went two legionnaires, clearing the crowd aside
as best they could, with curses and careless blows.
The procession moved at a snail's pace.
The soldiers tried to keep step.
The centurion's guard evidently did not relish this routine
task, which came to them every now and then in the
governing of this troublesome province.

The sunlight glanced on the spears and helmets of the
soldiers. There was a clanking of steel as their shields
touched their belt buckles and the scabbards of their swords.

Between the two files of soldiers staggered three condemned
men, each carrying a heavy bar of wood, with its cross-piece,
on which he was to be executed.

It was hard to keep step, for the pace was slow, and the
soldiers were impatient to get it over.
Left . . . right . . . left . . . right . . .

In sharp clipped commands they urged their prisoners on.

The crosses were heavy, and the first of the victims was at
the point of collapse.
He had been under severe strain for several days.
He had eaten little and had not closed his eyes for two days.

Moreover, he had been lashed with the scourge,

a leather whip with rough pieces of lead tied in every thong.

The carpenter followed them, with his ladder and his nails, and they all moved forward out of the courtyard of Pilate's palace and made for the gate leading out of the city.

The sun was hot. The sweat poured down the face of Jesus, and He swayed now and then under the weight of the cross. A depression had fallen on the soldiers, and they marched in silence, as if reluctantly.

A group of women went with the procession, their faces half-hidden by their veils, but their grief could not be hidden. Some were sobbing . . .
    Others were praying . . .
        Others were moaning in that deep grief that knows not what they say or do.

Some of them had children by the hand and kept saying over and over . . . "He gave my child back to me . . . How can they be so cruel? I know He healed my child—what harm could there be in that?"

And there were men, too, who followed as closely as they could—men who walked with the strange steps of men to whom walking was unfamiliar.
They were the cripples He had healed.

Others carried sticks in their hands,
sticks that once had tapped out their blind tattoo along the city streets and the sun-hardened trails of Judea.

They did not use their sticks now, although once again they were blind . . . blinded by tears.

Once when the procession halted for a moment. Jesus turned and spoke to them, but they could not hear Him for the shouting of the rabble.

Most of the crowd hardly knew what was going on.
They did not understand.
They caught the infection of the mob spirit.
They shouted to the first of the three victims.
That one had an absurd crown on His head,
twisted from a branch of the long-thorned briar.
It had lacerated His scalp and caused blood to mingle with the sweat.

They shouted at Him, until roughly pushed aside by the soldiers, and then in some cases, they began to shout at the soldiers. It was an ugly situation as the procession went slowly along this way which will forever be known as the Via Dolorosa.

Meanwhile—Simon of Cyrene was approaching the city gate.

He had just arrived in Judea, and was about to enter the Holy City, as a pilgrim for the festival.
He had spent the night in some village just outside, and, rising early this morning, had bathed and dressed himself carefully . . . with a tingling excitement because soon he would be in Jerusalem.

The wonders of Jerusalem that exiles had described, he would see with his own eyes.
The sounds of the Holy City which lonely hearts heard in their nostalgia . . .
Noises that seemed to be whispered by the restless surf of

distant seas, or heard in the moaning of winds that travelled
far . . .
These he would hear with his own ears.

Yet he tried to keep calm, and as he set out on the short
walk that lay between him and the city, he was very thoughtful.

He walked along the winding path that sometimes ran
through the fields . . .
    sometimes along the tortuous course of the dried-up
        river bed . . .
Sometimes it wound up the jagged hillside to twist down
among giant boulders and huge rocks behind which many a
robber might hide.
He walked along beside the tall rushes,
    and through the divided crops.

He could hear the sheep bleating on the inhospitable hillside,
while the morning sun climbed higher and chased away
the mists that lay in the hollows, trailing down into the
ravines like tulle scarfs.
As he walked along, he was thinking of the temple and its
glories, the history of his people and the worship of his
fathers . . .
Already he could see ahead of him the domes of the Temple
gleaming gold in the sunshine, and he thought of his own
city looking from her height over the blue waters of the
Mediterranean.

As he neared the city gate he began to hear shouting that
grew louder and louder.
There seemed to Simon to be a sort of chant running
through the noise . . . a refrain that men's voices made

clearer and clearer until he thought he could recognize the
words "Crucify
    crucify
      crucify . . ."
They met right at the city gate . . .
   Simon of Cyrene and the crowd.

He found that the procession was headed by some Roman
soldiers; he would recognize them anywhere . . .
    the insignia on their shields . . .
  and their uniforms . . .
He could tell a legionnaire when he saw one.

He had little time to gather impressions,
and as for asking questions, that was impossible.
He could not make himself heard in all the rabble.

The noise and confusion with its sinister malice made
Simon shudder.
Simon was aware of two moving walls of Roman steel,
between which there staggered a Man carrying a cross.

There was something strange about it all, but before he
could understand it, Simon was caught up in it—sucked
into the procession, and swept out through the gate again.

Simon was excited, afraid . . .
He was puzzled and ill at ease.
He scanned face after face quickly, looking for some
  light of pity . . .
    of friendliness,
      of welcome,
looking for a smile, but he found none.
There were no smiles.

He felt the drama of the situation,
   the cruelty of it . . . and its horror crept over him like a clammy mist—and he shivered.

He was captured by the procession, stumbling along tightly wedged in the very heart of the crowd.
Then he noticed that there were three men who staggered under the weight of crosses of rough, heavy wood on which these unfortunates were going to die.

Each man was bent beneath the burden he carried,
and perspiration moistened their drawn faces.
One of them was strangely appealing,
   His face was arresting.
Simon felt his gaze returning again and again to that one Face. He noticed that blood was trickling down from wounds in the brow.
On His head there was a twig of long-thorned briar, twisted around in the shape of a crown and pushed down cruelly on His head.

Simon watched with beating heart as they shuffled along, fascinated by the look in those eyes.
He could see nothing else. Everything was forgotten, even why he came to Jerusalem.

This public execution had driven everything else from his mind.
Forgotten for the moment was the Temple,
   and its services,
     messages he brought from friends far away . . .
      things he had been asked to get . . .
everything was forgotten as he watched this Man carrying the cross.

And then *He* looked up! His eyes almost blinded by the blood that trickled down from under that grotesque crown that was on His head . . .

Why didn't somebody wipe His eyes?

And as Simon looked at Him; He looked at Simon . . . and the eyes of the two . . . met!

How did Christ know what was in Simon's heart?
What was it that made Him smile, a slow, sad smile that seemed to still Simon's wildly beating heart and give him courage?

The look that passed between them Simon never forgot as long as he lived, for no man can look at Jesus of Nazareth and remain the same.

As these two looked at each other, the Man with the cross stumbled, and the soldiers, moved more by impatience than pity, seeing that the Nazarene was almost too exhausted to carry the cross any farther, laid hands on Simon and conscripted him to carry it.

He was the nearest man.
He was strong.
His shoulders were broad!

Simon's heart almost stopped beating. He tried to speak, but no words came.
A few minutes before, he had been a lonely pilgrim quietly approaching the Holy City.
And now, there he was in the midst of a procession of howling men and women,
walking between two moving walls of Roman steel,

and carrying on his shoulder a cross on which someone was going to die!

The look of gratitude and love that flashed from the eyes of Jesus as Simon lifted the load from those tired, bleeding shoulders did something to the man from Cyrene, and in an instant life was changed.

Simon never could explain it afterwards . . .
    how it happened!
There are moments of spiritual insight that defy the limits of syntax and grammar.
There are experiences that can never be poured into the moulds of speech.
There are some things too deep for words.

But all at once he saw the meaning of pain . . .
    understood the significance of suffering . . .
The meaning of prayer was unveiled . . .
    and the message of the Scriptures.
He saw prophecy take form and live before him.
He remembered words of the psalmist and the prophets of old, words that until now had been without sense or meaning, but now . . . he saw . . . and understood.

And so they came to Calvary, a hill shaped like a skull, outside the city gates,
where two great highways converged upon Jerusalem.
This hill was the usual place of execution.

Only as the nails were driven in, did the shouting stop.
There was a hush.
    Most of them were stunned . . . horrified . . .
Even the hardest of them was silenced,

H

and the thud of the hammer was faintly re-echoed from the city walls.

Mary, the mother of Jesus, stopped her ears and closed her eyes. She could not bear the thud of the hammer.
Simon of Cyrene from time to time wiped away his tears with the back of his hand.
Peter stood on the fringe of the crowd blinded by hot tears that filled his eyes, while his very heart broke.

They hurled His own words back at Him, but they were barbs, dipped in venom and shot from snarling lips, like poisoned arrows.

"He saved others, Himself He cannot save.
Yes, He healed the cripples.
Yes, He gave sight to the blind.
He made withered arms whole again.
He even brought back the dead, but He cannot save Himself".

"Perform a miracle now, Miracle Man! Come down from the Cross, and we will believe you.
Aha, Thou who wouldest build the temple in three days.
Thou hast nails in Thy hands . . .
Thou hast wood . . . go on and build Thy temple".

"If thou be the Christ . . . come on down from the Cross!"

They shouted until they were hoarse.
The noise was so great that only a few of them standing near the Cross heard what He said when His lips moved in prayer:

112

"Father, forgive them, for they know not what they do".

One of the thieves, drugged and half drunk, cried out to Jesus:
"Can't you see how we suffer?
If you are the Son of God, take us down from these crosses. Save us and yourself".

Then a spasm of pain gripped him, and he began to curse and to swear, blaming Jesus for the pain.

But the other turned his head, so that he could see Jesus, and he said to his companion:
"Dost thou not fear God, seeing thou art in the same condemnation? And we indeed justly, for we have broken their laws . . . but this man hath done nothing amiss".

Then he said to Jesus: "Remember me when thou comest into thy kingdom".
And Jesus, His face drawn with pain, but His voice still kind, answered:
"This very day when this pain is over, we shall be together . . . you and I . . . in Paradise".
And the man, comforted, set his lips to endure to the end.

The sun rose higher and higher. Time oozed out like the blood that dripped from the Cross . . .
Jesus opened His eyes and saw His mother standing there, and John beside her.
He called out the name of John, who came closer, and Jesus said:
"You will take care of her, John?" . . .

113

and John, choked with tears, put his arm round the shoulders of Mary.

Jesus said to His mother: "He will be your son".
His lips were parched, and He spoke with difficulty.
He moved His head uneasily against the hard wood of the Cross, as a sick man moves his head on a hot pillow.

The women beneath the Cross stood praying for Jesus and for the thieves.
The centurion was silent, although every now and then he would look up at Jesus with a strange look on his face.
The soldiers were silent, too. Their gambling was done.
    They had won . . . and lost.

Suddenly Jesus opened His eyes and gave a loud cry.
The gladness in His voice startled all who heard it, for it sounded like a shout of victory:
    "It is finished. Father, into thy hands I commit my spirit."

And with that cry He died.

They were all there that day. The friends of Jesus
        and His enemies
    The church people
as well as those who never went to church.
The priests
    the scribes
        the greedy Sadducees
            the hypocrites
                and the proud Pharisees—
they were all there.

The people who were always talking about the church and

praying in public—they were there.
The unbelievers
     the gamblers
          the harlots and their customers, they were there.

Simon of Cyrene
     and the soldiers—they were there.
Peter was there
     and John
          and Andrew, and the other disciples.
They were all there . . .

"Were you there when they crucified my Lord?
Were you there when they crucified my Lord?
Oh! Sometimes it causes me to tremble, tremble, tremble.
Were you there when they crucified my Lord?"⁹

Were *you* there when they crucified my Lord?

When we consider who were there, and when we are honest
with ourselves, we know that we were there,
and that we helped to put Jesus on His cross!

Every attitude present on that hilltop that day, is present in
our midst now!

Every emotion that tugged at human hearts then, tugs at
human hearts now.
Every face that was there, is here too.
Every voice that shouted then is shouting still.
Every human being was represented on Calvary.
Every sin was in a nail
     or a spear
  or a thorn

and pardon for them all in the blood that was shed!

More than nineteen hundred years have passed . . .
The Cross itself has long since crumbled into dust.
Yet it stands again when we choose our own Calvary and
crucify Him all over again, with every sin of commission
and omission.

   Every wrong attitude . . .
  every bad disposition . . .
 every unkind word . . .
  every impure imagination . . .
   every ignoble desire . . .
    every unworthy ambition . . .

Yes, Calvary still stands, and the crowd at the top of the hill.

Were you there when they crucified my Lord?
I was . . . Were you?

Prayer

God of our fathers and our God, give us the faith to believe in the ultimate triumph of righteousness . . . We pray for the bifocals of faith that see the despair and the need of the hour but also see, further on, the patience of our God working out His plan in the world He has made . . . Through Jesus our Lord. AMEN.

The Resurrection never becomes a fact of experience until the risen Christ lives in the heart of the believer.

From I HAVE THE KEYS

The Verdict Of The Empty Tomb

S o much had happened in those last few days.
To Cleopas and his friend, the week that had closed
seemed like a terrible dream.

Event had followed event in a swiftness which had left no
time for meditation.
As the two men walked along the winding road to Emmaus,
it was of these things they spoke.

There had been Christ's entry in triumph into the Holy City.
To all of them, it had seemed that—at last—their Messiah
would enter into His own.
Surely, now the days of Roman occupation would soon be
over.
Exactly when the Messiah would announce Himself and
declare their independence, they did not know.
Joyously, the multitudes thronged around Him, awaiting the
good news.

Then, swiftly, there had been woven around the Nazarene
a net of intrigue—soon to be drawn tighter and tighter.

There had been the slamming of a door on that night when
Judas went out to keep his treacherous rendezvous.
There had been Jesus' strange words of dismissal, as He
watched Judas disappear into the darkness of the night.

119

Then the scene that followed in the garden out on the hillside . . .
Would they ever forget it?
In the silence of the night, Jesus prostrate in prayer . . .
  the bright Syrian stars seeming to fill all the sky . . .
  the gnarled olive trees casting grotesque shadows . . .
  a swinging lantern coming up the winding path . . .
 the rabble of temple door-keepers and temple police,
who had laid aside their brooms and their keys long enough
to come out with Judas to arrest the Galilean . . .
How could they ever forget?

As Cleopas and his companion talked, they became more and more engrossed.
Their words came pouring out in a torrent of recollection.

There had been the despicable kiss of Judas . . .
 the arrest itself . . .
the foolhardiness of Peter with his little sword . . .
 the return to the city . . .
  Peter's blasphemous denial by the fire . . .
  the all-night vigil.

The rest was an agony of painful memories . . .
 the scourging of Christ in front of Pilate's palace . . .
  the blood-thirsty cries of the mob . . .
   the march to Golgotha . . .
    those awful moments, when the sound of a hammer
had echoed across the valley.

There had been the ravings and curses of the thieves on
their crosses . . .
 the strange eerie darkness . . .
  and the earthquake . . .

120

and the death of Him whom they had learned to love,
of Him whom they called Master.

He had died after only six hours of suffering.
Long enough surely . . .
Yet the Roman centurion who watched could not believe
that any crucified one could die in just six hours.
To make sure, one of the soldiers had pierced Christ's side
with a spear, and the last remaining drops of His blood
were poured out.

It was plain to be seen that the Nazarene was dead.
There was no need to break His legs in an effort to hasten
death.

"That one didn't take long", they said, as they prepared to
fall in line and march back to their barracks.
"It is rumoured around that this One actually said He would
rise from the dead. Now He's dead, just like any other dead
man".

So it was that the Jewish leaders went to Pilate to ask him
for a watch of soldiers around the tomb for three days.
They were not willing to run any risk that Jesus' disciples
would steal His body away, and then insist that He *had*
risen again.

Pilate granted their request saying:
"Ye have a watch, go your way, make it as sure as you
can".

They had a huge stone rolled across the entrance to the cave.
This they sealed with their own official seal, as Matthew
said,

"So they went and made the sepulchre sure, sealing the stone and setting a watch".

This, they felt sure, was a sure guarantee against any fraud. A broken seal would reveal that the grave had been opened from the outside, but the soldiers would be on guard to prevent that happening.

So engrossed were the two men in these memories, that they did not notice the approach of a stranger.

Suddenly, there He was walking beside them.[10]

And He said to them, "What is this conversation which you are holding with each other as you walk?"

And they stood still, looking sad. Then one of them, named Cleopas, answered him,

"Are you the only visitor to Jerusalem who does not know the things that have happened there in these days?"

And He said to them, "What things?"

And they said to Him, "Concerning Jesus of Nazareth, who was a prophet mighty in deed and word before God and all the people, and how our chief priests and rulers delivered Him up to be condemned to death and crucified Him. But we had hoped that He was the one to redeem Israel. Yes, and besides all this, it is now the third day since this happened.

"Moreover, some women of our company amazed us. They were at the tomb early in the morning and did not find his body; and they came back saying that they had even seen a vision of angels, who said that He was alive . . . But Him they did not see".

And He said to them, "O foolish men, and slow of heart to believe all that the prophets have spoken! Was it not necessary that the Christ should suffer these things and enter into his glory?"

And He began with Moses and all the prophets and explained to them all the Scriptures that referred to Himself.

Thus did the walk of seven and a half miles pass quickly. And when they reached Emmaus, the sun was fast sinking behind copper hills.
The shadows were long . . .
    Soon it would be dark.

The two men begged the mysterious Stranger to spend the night with them, or at least to share their evening meal.
Still they did not know who He was.
Why?
Partly because Christ was the last person these disciples expected to see. Had they not seen Him die?
Had they not watched His head fall limp on His shoulders?

It had seemed so absurd to them as they stood at the foot of the Cross and remembered His words:
    "Whosoever believeth in Me, though he were dead, yet shall he live . . . and whosoever liveth and believeth in Me shall never die . . ."

Then to see Him die—right there before their eyes . . .

They had not been able to grasp the glorious truth that life hereafter is not dependent upon the physical at all . . .
    is not material but spiritual.
So the disciples imagined that Jesus of Nazareth could not

possibly be alive unless He were just as He was before . . .
dependent upon the same material limitations that
bounded their lives.

And so they sat down at last to eat their evening meal.
The Stranger stayed with them, and in the most natural
way in the world, gave thanks before He took bread in His
hands.

There was something in the way He gave thanks . . .
As He took bread . . .
reached across the table . . .
broke the bread with a characteristic gesture . . .
and the folds of His robe fell back . . .
Perhaps they saw the livid red marks of the nails in His
hands . . . but whatever it was, in that instant they knew
Him
. . . and He was gone.

It wasn't possible!
It couldn't be . . .
Then the women were right!
They had seen Him with their own eyes.
And they rose and ran—ran, not walked, all the seven and a
half miles back to Jerusalem to tell the other disciples the
incredible news.

Implicit in this incident is the fact that the disciples did not
expect this to happen.
Their belief in the Resurrection was not some fantastic idea
wafted in from the swamps of their fevered imaginations.

It was not some romantic wish out of their dream-house, not
the result of wishful thinking,

for it came as a complete shock,
  unexpected
    bewildering.

John and Peter, as they had gone into the grave in the garden that first Easter morning, did not know *what* to think—until they saw what was inside the grave—
  and then they believed.

The inside of the tomb revealed something that proved the Resurrection. What was it?
Let us turn to the narrative again and read carefully:

> "Then cometh Simon Peter following him, and went into the sepulchre, and seeth the linen clothes lie. And the napkin, that was about his head, not lying with the linen clothes, but wrapped together in a place by itself. Then went in also that other disciple, which came first to the sepulchre, and he saw, and believed." (JOHN 20 : 6-8).

In this connection, it is well for us to remember that the stone was rolled away from the door, not to permit Christ to come out, but to enable the disciples to go in.

Notice what it was they saw.
They saw the linen clothes lying, not unwound and carefully folded, as some people appear to think—
  not thrown aside as is a covering when one rises from bed, but lying there on the stone slab in the shape of the body.

True, the napkin had been removed and folded, but the grave-clothes were lying there, mute but eloquent evidence that a living organism had come out.

The grave-clothes lay like the shrivelled, cracked shell of a cocoon, left behind when the moth has emerged and hoisted her bright sails in the sunshine . . .
or, more accurately, like a glove from which the hand has been removed, the fingers of which still retain the shape of the hand.

In that manner, the grave-clothes were lying, collapsed a little—slightly deflated—because there was between the rolls of bandages a considerable weight of spices, but there lay the linen cloth that had been wound round the body of Christ.

It was when they saw *that*, that the disciples believed.

The Greek word here for "see" is not to behold as one looks at a spectacle, not to see as the watch-maker who peers through his magnifying glass.
It means to see with inner sight that leads one to a conclusion.

It is perception
    reflection
        understanding—more than sight.
Do you *see?*

It is to see, as one who reasons from the effect to the cause, and when John and Peter reasoned from what they saw in the tomb, they arrived at the conclusion
        the unshakable
    unassailable
  certain conviction
that Jesus Christ had risen from the dead.

Then, what happened?

Suddenly Peter is facing the foes of Jesus with a reckless courage.

He speaks boldly:

"Ye men of Israel, hear these words; Jesus of Nazareth, a man approved of God among you by miracles and wonders and signs, which God did by him in the midst of you, as ye yourselves also know:

Him, being delivered by the determinate counsel and foreknowledge of God, ye have taken, and by wicked hands have crucified and slain:

Whom God hath raised up, having loosed the pains of death: because it was not possible that he should be holden of it". (ACTS 2 : 22-24).

Why, this does not sound like the same man. The truth is, it is not the same man. He is different—

very, very different.

What had happened?

The undeniable fact is this: the disciples of Jesus were
       scattered
      downcast
    hopeless
with a sense of tragic loss
and then, in a few days, they were thrilling with victory, completely changed.

There is no more adamant fact in the records than the changes that came over these men.

When their Master was arrested, they had all either fled or followed at a great distance.

Peter was so fearful that he had denied ever even having known the Nazarene.

After Jesus' death, the band of disciples stayed in hiding—
with the doors locked—"for fear of the Jews".

Yet, after Christ's Resurrection, we find these same timid
    frightened
  ineffective men
preaching openly, apparently with no fear of anyone,
"turning the world upside down".

They suffered imprisonment
  threats
    scourgings
      persecutions
        stonings and death.
Nothing could silence them.

Now it takes a very great conviction to change men so
drastically. Nor do men persist in a lie or even a delusion, if
every time they insist on its truth, they are driving nails
into their own coffins.

Men do not invent a story,
so that they can be crucified upside down, like Peter . . .
  or have their head chopped off, like Paul, outside the city
  of Rome,
    or be stoned to death—like Stephen.

A self-hypnotic illusion may sustain men for a time—but not
for long. In the long run, an illusion does not build character
strong enough to stand great hardship,
  great persecution.
Only the truth can do that!

Moreover, men who are merely fooling themselves do not

become purposeful men
   well-integrated men
      with self-sustaining qualities of leadership . . .
as these erstwhile timid apostles became.

And so here is the second fact—It was their continuing
fellowship with their Risen Lord through the years which
became the integrating
   guiding
      sustaining
power of their lives.

Through His spirit they had guidance and strength . . .

They had His wisdom
   His peace
      and His joy.
         They had boldness and courage
            and they had power . . .
qualities that they did not have until after that first Easter
morning.

They felt that they still were in touch with Him . . .
in a different way—yes—but in a more powerful way.

They knew that He was still with them, even as He had
promised . . .
   "Go ye into the world and lo, I am with you always".

They felt that! They knew it!
The promises He had made to them before His death were
now fulfilled, and they (men like Cleopas and his friend)
went up and down in the land . . .
   they crossed the sea . . .

They shook the Roman Empire until it tottered and fell.
They changed the world.

That is the fact you can't ignore.

Through the nineteen centuries which have followed in
every land there have been men and women who have
experienced the same fellowship . . .
    who have felt the same power in their lives . . .
        who have had the same peace and inner serenity . . .
           who have had the same joy
               the same radiant victory.

They are not crackpots
   morons
      or lunatics.
Included among them are some of the greatest minds the
world has ever seen . . .
some of the most brilliant thinkers
      philosophers
    scientists
  and scholars . . .
They were not frustrated personalities who fled the world of
reality and found refuge in the dug-outs of their own wistful
escapes from life.

On the contrary, most of them have been radiant souls
filled with an abiding joy, living to the full every golden
hour, and tasting the deepest joys of life.

Dismiss, as you will, the sentimentality, the hysteria and the
wishful thinking that may be born in times of crisis and
danger, there is still a residue of hard stubborn testimony
from men who met Him during the Second World War . . .

For example, while they drifted on life-rafts on the ocean . . .
who came home through dangerous skies "on a wing and a
prayer" . . .who met Him in the dog-watch of many a long
night in dangerous waters.

And you, too, may have that fellowship with the Risen
Christ.
You, too, may have in your own life that sense of His
nearness and His power.

Your life today may be guided by Christ . . .
Your problems may be solved by His wisdom . . .
   Your weaknesses may be turned into strength
      by His help . . .
         Your struggles may become victories by His grace . . .
Your sorrows may be turned into joy by His comfort.

To you there may come the same wonderful changes that
have come to other men and women all down through the
years.

This is a reality that can be yours.
   To the man in the street . . .
      to the government clerk . . .
         to the anxious mother . . .
            to the confused school boy or girl
this comradeship with the Resurrected Christ through His
spirit is available now.

This is the real meaning of Easter.
Forget the bunny rabbit and the coloured eggs.
Forget the symbols of spring that so often confuse and
conceal the real meaning of what we celebrate on that day.

No tabloid will ever print the startling news that the mummified body of Jesus of Nazareth has been discovered in old Jerusalem.

Christians have no carefully embalmed body enclosed in a glass case by which to worship.

Thank God, we have an empty tomb.

The glorious fact that the empty tomb proclaims to us is that life for us does not stop when death comes.

Death is not a wall, but a door.

And eternal life which may be ours now, by faith in Christ, is not interrupted when the soul leaves the body,

    for we live on . . . and on.

There is no death to those who have entered into fellowship with Him who emerged from the tomb.

Because the Resurrection is true, it is the most significant thing in our world today.

Bringing the Resurrected Christ into our lives, individual and national, is the only hope we have for making a better world.

    "Because I live, ye shall live also."

That is the message of Easter.

Prayer

We pray to Thee, O Christ, to keep us under the spell of immortality.

May we never again think and act as if Thou wert dead. Let us more and more come to know Thee as a living Lord who hath promised to them that believe: "Because I live, ye shall live also."

Help us to remember that we are praying to the Conqueror of Death, that we may no longer be afraid nor be dismayed by the world's problems and threats, since Thou hast overcome the world.

In Thy strong name, we ask for Thy living presence and Thy victorious power.
AMEN.

Man cannot comprehend Infinity. Yet the crumb of our pity comes from the whole loaf of God's compassion. The milk of human kindness comes from the dairies of God's love.

From THE LOCKED DOOR

By Invitation Of Jesus

Then said he also to him that bade him, When thou makest a dinner or a supper, call not thy friends, nor thy brethren, neither thy kinsmen, nor thy rich neighbours; lest they also bid thee again, and a recompence be made thee.

But when thou makest a feast, call the poor, the maimed, the lame, the blind:

And thou shalt be blessed; for they cannot recompense thee: for thou shalt be recompensed at the resurrection of the just. LUKE 14 : 12, 13, 14.

SUPPOSE SOMEONE in Washington living far out on Massachusetts Avenue
or in Spring Valley
happened one day to open a Bible and, by that mysterious process known only to angels, chanced to read these verses in the Gospel of Luke.

Suppose the reader concluded that these words, probably spoken in Aramaic so long ago beneath a Syrian sky, were just as applicable in the twentieth-century society.

Suppose that person believed that the blessings Jesus mentioned were worth having and decided to claim them. Suppose he had the courage and the love that would be

135

required to take Jesus at His word. What do you think would happen?

One bitterly cold night, when Washington was covered with a blanket of snow and ice, a man sat in his home on Massachusetts Avenue.
The house was very comfortable . . .
A crackling log fire in the fireplace threw dancing shadows on the panelled walls.
The wind outside was moaning softly like someone in pain, and the reading-lamp cast a soft warm glow on the Book this man was reading.

He was alone, for the children had gone to the Shoreham for supper and dancing, and his wife had retired early after a strenuous afternoon's bridge game.

He read the passage of Luke which is our text, and then could read no more.

Somehow he could not get away from those simple words. He had read the Bible often, for he was a good man, but never before did the words seem printed in flame.

He closed the Bible, and sat musing, conscious for the first time in his life of the challenge of Christ.

He felt as though Someone were standing behind him; he knew he was no longer alone.

What strange fancy was this?
Why was it that he kept hearing—in a whisper—the words he had just read?

"I must be sleepy and dreamy", he thought to himself, "it is time I went to bed".

But it was long ere he fell asleep, for still the voice whispered and still he was conscious of a Presence in the room.

He could not shake it off.
Never before had he been so challenged.
He thought of the dinners and parties that they had given in this beautiful home.

He thought of those whom he usually invited.
Most of them were listed in "Who's Who in Washington"; and there were those whose names were household names in business
    finance
       clubs
          and in government circles.
There were men with the power to grant political and social favours.

But *they* were not poor
    or maimed
      or lame
        or blind.

What had put this absurd thought into his head anyhow?
He tried to sleep, but somehow he could not close the door of his mind to the procession that shuffled and tapped its way down the corridors of his soul.

There were beggars with trembling lips.
There were sightless eyes that stared straight in front and faces blue with cold.
There were sticks tapping on the pavement.

137

There were crutches that creaked with the weight of a twisted body.

As he watched them pass, he felt his own heart touched.
He whispered a prayer that if the Lord would give him courage, he would take Him at His word and do what He wanted him to do.
Only then did he find peace and fall asleep.

When the morning came, his determination gave him new strength and zest for the day.
He must begin his preparations
  and he was impatient to go downtown.

His first call was on the engraver who knew him well.
At the counter he drafted the card he wished engraved,
  chuckling now and then as he wrote, his eyes shining.
The clerk who read the card looked somewhat puzzled but made no comment, although he stood watching the retreating form swing down the street.

The card read:

JESUS OF NAZARETH
Requests the honour of your presence
at a banquet honouring
The Sons of Want
on Friday evening, in a home on Massachusetts Avenue
Cars will await you at the Central Union Mission
at six o'clock

"COME UNTO ME, ALL YE THAT LABOUR AND ARE HEAVY LADEN, AND I WILL GIVE YOU REST."

In the engraving room, they did not know what to make of it;

but the conclusion they reached was that someone had more money than sense, but that it was none of their business.

A few days later, with the cards of invitation in his hand, he walked downtown and gave them out, and within an hour there were several people wondering what could be the meaning of the card that a kindly
    happy
  well-dressed man
had placed in their hands.

There was the old man seated on a box trying to sell pencils; and another on the corner with a racking cough and a bundle of papers under his arms.

There was a blind man saying over and over to himself, "Jesus of Nazareth requests the honour of your presence".

A fellow who was fingering a gun in his pocket and bitterly thinking of suicide wondered whether he should wait until night.

Because he had a sense of humour, this good man called the newspapers and was connected with the writers of the society column. To them he announced the banquet that was to be given in his home that night, and asked if perhaps they would like to make mention of it or have some pictures made.

Because his name was an impressive one,
    because he was rich and influential in Washington business and politics,
he met with an enthusiastic response.

When he was asked the names of his guests, he simply said:
    "I do not know their names; I have not asked them".

Somewhat puzzled, the editor of the society column laughed, thinking that he was joking,
but she was even more puzzled when this man laughed and said: "If you care to come out tonight, I promise you a unique experience".

At six o'clock, a strange group of men stood waiting in the vestibule of the Central Union Mission, talking softly together.

"What is the catch in this, anyhow?" asked one cynical fellow.
"What's the game?"
  "Who's throwing this feed?
  Anybody know the bird what gave out the tickets?"

"Well, what difference does it make?
  I'd stand almost anything for a feed."

And the blind man, with the little boy at his side, ventured to remark: "Maybe it's part of the government relief programme".
And the cynic was saying, "Aw, somebody's kiddin' us, as if we weren't wretched enough already".

Just then someone came over and announced that the cars were at the door; without a word, they went outside.

Perhaps there was something incongruous about it all, seeing these men, clutching their thin coats tightly around their thin bodies,
    huddling together, their faces pinched and wan
      blue with cold and unshaven

their toes sticking out of their shoes, climbing into two shiny limousines.
It was touching to see the lame get in, dragging one foot, swinging up with a twitch of pain,
 and to see the blind man fumbling for the strap.

At last they were all inside, and the cars glided off with the strangest and most puzzled load of passengers they had ever carried.

When they dismounted, they stood gazing at the house, its broad steps and lamps
 its thick-piled carpets.
They entered slowly, trying to take it all in.
They were met by the host, a little nervous, but smiling.

He was a quiet man, and they liked him—these guests of his whose names he did not know.
He did not say much, only, "I am so glad you came".

By and by, they were seated at the table.
They had looked at the tapestries that hung on the walls.
They had seen the illuminated pictures in their massive frames, and the giant crystal chandelier,
 the concert grand piano that stood across the hall,
 the spotless linen, and the gleaming silver on the table.

They were silent now; even the cynic had nothing to say.
It seemed as if the banquet would be held in frozen silence.

The host rose in his place, and in a voice that trembled slightly said: "My friends, let us ask the blessing".

 "If this is pleasing to Thee, O Lord, bless us as we sit

around this table, and bless the food that we are about
to receive.
Bless these men. You know who they are, and what
they need.
And help us to do what you want us to do.
Accept our thanks, in Jesus' name. Amen."

The blind man was smiling now.
He turned to the man seated next to him and asked him
about the host.
"What does he look like?"

And so the ice was broken; conversation began to stir
around the table, and soon the first course was laid.

"My friends, I hope you will enjoy the dinner.
I would suggest that we waste no time, for I have no doubt
that you are hungry. Go right ahead."

It was a strange party, rather fantastic in a way, thought the
host, as he surveyed his guests.

There they were—men who otherwise might be still
loitering on the back streets of Washington
    crouched in doorways
        or huddled over some watchman's fire.

What an amazing thing that he didn't even know the name
of a single man!
His guests had no credentials
    no social recommendations
        no particular graces—so far as he could see.
But, my, they were hungry!

It was funny, as he sat there talking, how the stories in the
Gospels kept coming back to him, and he could almost
imagine that the house was one in Jerusalem.

It seemed to him that these men would be the very ones
that Jesus would have gathered around Him—the legion
of the world's wounded,
   the fraternity of the friendless
      pieces of broken human earthenware.

He remembered what the family had said . . .
How they had insisted on demanding, "Why? Why are you
doing such a thing?"
Well why was it, anyway?
   Wasn't it plain?

His reason was the same old glorious reason that Jesus had
for every miracle
   for every gesture of love
      for every touch of healing.
It was simply because he was sorry for these people, and because
he wanted to do this one thing on an impulse of love.

Yet there was not a trace of condescension in his attitude.
He was treating them as brothers, talking to them as though
they had a right to be sitting where they were.

It was a grand feeling—a great adventure.
Never before in his life had he felt this thrill.
These men could not pay him back!
   What had they to give him?

He watched each plate and directed the servants with a nod
or a glance.

K

He encouraged them to eat;
 he laughed at their thinly disguised reluctance,
 until they laughed too.
As he sat there, it suddenly occurred to him how different
was the conversation!

There were no off-colour stories, no whisperings of scandal,
no one saying, "Well, I have it on good authority".

They were talking about their friends in misfortune, wish-
ing they were here too . . .
 wondering whether Charlie had managed to get a bed in
 the charity ward
  whether Dick had stuck it out when he wanted to end
  it all, whether the little woman with the baby had
  got a job.

Wasn't the steak delicious!
And they marvelled that they still remembered how different
foods tasted.
They wondered, most of all, who this man was, and why he
had invited them all here.

When the meal was over, there was music.
Someone came in and sat down at the piano.

He began to play softly, familiar melodies, old songs;
and then in a soft, but understanding voice, he began to
sing.
They listened to "Love's Old Sweet Song"
   "Silver Threads Among the Gold"
  and then a march by Sousa
  and then "Traumerei"
 and then "The Sidewalks of New York".

Someone else joined in—a cracked, wheezing voice, but it
started the others.
Men who had not sung for months
    men who had no reason to sing
there they were, joining in.

Now some old favourites: "Daisy"
    "A Bicycle Built for Two"
    "Swanee River".
Soon they began to request this and that, and before they
knew it, they were singing hymns:
    "What a Friend We Have in Jesus"
        "The Church in the Wildwood"
            "When I Survey the Wondrous Cross".

The pianist stopped, and the guests grouped themselves in
soft, comfortable chairs around the log fire; some of them
smoked.

The host moved among them, smiling . . . his eyes shining.
Then when he had settled himself again, and his guests were
comfortable, he said:
    "I know you men are wondering what all this means.
    I can tell you very simply.
    But, first, let me read you something."

He read from the Gospels stories of One who moved among
the sick
    the outcasts
        the despised and the friendless,
how He healed this one
    cured that one
        spoke kindly words of infinite meaning to another,
            how He visited the ostracized

145

and what He promised to all who believed in Him.

"Now I haven't done much tonight for you, but it has made me very happy to have you here in my home.
I hope you have enjoyed it half as much as I have.
If I have given you one evening of happiness, I shall be forever glad to remember it, and you are under no obligation to me.
This is not my party. It is His!
I have merely lent Him this house.
He was your *Host*. He is your *Friend*.
And He has given me the honour of speaking for Him.

"He wants you all to have a good time.
He is sad when you are.
   He hurts when you do.
      He weeps when you weep.
He wants to help you, if you will let Him.

"I'm going to give each of you His Book of Instructions.
I have marked certain passages in it that you will find help-ful when you are sick and in pain
      when you are lonely and discouraged
         when you are blue and bitter and hopeless
            and when you lose a loved one.
He will speak a message of hope and courage and faith.

"Then I shall see each one of you tomorrow where I saw you today, and we'll have a talk together to see just how I can help you most.

"I have made arrangements for each one of you to get back to your homes, and those who have nowhere to go, I invite to spend the night here."

146

They shuffled out into the night, a different group from what they had been.
There was a new light in their eyes
a smile where there had not been even interest before.

The blind man was smiling still, and as he stood on the doorstep, waiting, he turned to where his host stood.
"God bless you, my friend, whoever you are."

A little wizened fellow who had not spoken all night paused to say,
"I'm going to try again, mister; there's somethin' worth livin' for."

The cynic turned back, "Mister, you're the first man who ever gave me anything. And you've given me hope".

"That is because I was doing it for Him", said the host and he stood and waved good night as the cars purred off into the darkness.

When they had gone, he sat again by the fire and looked at the dying embers, until the feeling became overwhelming again that there was Someone in the room.

He could never tell anyone how he knew this, but he knew that He was smiling and that He approved.
And that night, on Massachusetts Avenue, a rich man smiled in his sleep.

And one who stood in the shadows smiled too,
because some of the least of these had been treated like brothers for His sake.

Of course, that never happened.
It is only a piece of imagination.
But why shouldn't it happen, on Massachusetts Avenue in Washington?
on Park Avenue in New York?
in Druid Hills in Atlanta?
on the Gold Coast in Chicago?
in Beverly Hills in Los Angeles?
I wonder what would happen if we all agreed to read one of the Gospels, until we came to a place that told us to do something, *then went out to do it*, and only after we had done it . . . began reading again?

Why don't we do what Jesus says?
How exciting life would become were we to begin living according to His way of life!

Friends would say we had lost our minds—perhaps.
Acquaintances would say we were "peculiar".
Those who dislike us would say we were crazy.

But Someone Else, who had these same things said about Him, would smile, and the joy and peace in our own hearts would tell us who was right.

There are aspects of the Gospel that are puzzling and difficult to understand.
But our problems are not centred around the things we don't understand, but rather in the things we do understand,
the things we could not possibly misunderstand.

This, after all, is but an illustration of the fact that our problem is not so much that we don't know what we should do.

We know perfectly well . . . but *we don't want to do it.*

Prayer

Forgive us, Lord Jesus, for doing the things that make us uncomfortable and guilty when we pray.

We say that we believe in God, and yet we doubt God's promises.

We say that in God we trust, yet we worry and try to manage our own affairs.

We say that we love Thee, O Lord, and yet do not obey Thee.

We believe that Thou hast the answers to all our problems, and yet we do not consult Thee.

Forgive us, Lord, for our lack of faith and the wilful pride that ignores the way, the truth, and the life.

Wilt Thou reach down and change the gears within us that we may go forward with Thee. AMEN.

149

Religion, you say, has broken down? Well, it may be that your puny prejudices, your preconceived ideas, your home-made theories and selfish philosophies have broken down—and that's a good thing. But that's not religion.

Perhaps you have seen that the ballyhoo and bunk that previously passed for religion aren't worth anything, and that's a splendid discovery to make. But real religion—experimental knowledge and worship of a personal God—communion with a risen Christ in a Spirit-directed life; hearts consecrated to Jesus Christ; lives motivated by the principles of the Great Galilean—these things are still here, just as regnant and as real as ever.

There is a great difference between the failure of a conception and the failure of the reality itself.

From SINGING IN THE RAIN

Mr Jones, Meet The Master

A minister was recently asked to make a patriotic address at a dinner attended by many men prominent in government and business, and by high-ranking military officials.

It was a swank affair, and cocktails and champagne were flowing freely.
Mr Jones—immediately to the minister's left—was a big name in steel.
He was—quite obviously—greatly enjoying the champagne.

"Best champagne I've had in many a day", he said. "Wonder where they rounded it up."

And then, suddenly noticing the still untouched glass before the minister's place—
"Say, you haven't touched yours . . . why not?
Guess I'm rude to mention it, but surely you haven't any scruples against champagne?"

The minister smiled. "No, you're not rude to ask, but it might take me a couple of minutes to answer you fully.
Are you asking out of curiosity, or just to make conversation . . .
    or because you really want to know?"

Mr Jones appeared somewhat startled by the minister's

151

candour.

"Say, now you do have my curiosity aroused.

I'm asking because I'd really like to know.

Everybody I know drinks.

What objection could there possibly be to a little champagne?"

The minister finished spreading a bit of butter on his roll before answering . . .

"Weekdays", he said, "I have a steady stream of people who need help coming to my study in the church.

Their lives are all messed up, and I guess you'd be surprised to know how often liquor is involved in the mess.

"They're from every walk of life
     rich and poor
   young and old
 men and women.

They look at me across my desk, and calmly . . . usually these days, without any sense of guilt or conviction of sin at all . . . tell me things awful enough to rock a man back on his heels.

"I hear the most fashionably dressed young women, and well-dressed men, tell stories of sordidness
    of moral filth
   of promiscuity
 even violence
which not even furs
  Cartier jewels
   or Prince Matchabelli perfume
could gloss over or make lovely.

"I hear these stories, until I have come to the place where,

watching the faces of passers-by, as I walk along the street,
I wonder if anywhere in this country there is any real
decency
  and honesty
     and purity walking around on two legs.

"I hear these stories, and I don't have to delve very deep
into any one of them to find that liquor in some form—
sometimes a very fashionable form—has aided and abetted
this moral chaos.
"I believe it's one of the most potent weapons the Devil
has in America today."

He paused . . . "Are you quite sure you want to hear all
of this?"

Mr Jones nodded, "Of course I do . . . if for no other
reason than that I haven't heard anybody talk like this
since I was a boy.
But I fail to see what all this has to do with not drinking
that glass of champagne."
The minister stirred his coffee slowly and thoughtfully . . .
"I was coming to that.
That's what I meant, when I said I couldn't answer your
question very briefly.

"Well, to continue . . . It seems to me that behind every
sin
  every vice
     every mess
is a lack of self-discipline . . . of God's discipline.

"I heard somebody say the other day that the future of our

world is going to be in the hands of disciplined people.
That's true.
The German people were disciplined, disciplined by their
Nazi overlords, and they almost succeeded in getting the
world in their hands.

"In a democracy, citizens have to be self-disciplined, or the
country goes down, defeated from within by moral rot.
That was undoubtedly why France fell.

"I'm beginning to see that if I, and others like me, are to
help people . . . really help, we, too, are going to have to
be disciplined in small ways as well as big.

"There's going to have to be a total lack of compromise. I
think liquor is one of our greatest problems.
It is a problem that has every thoughtful American worried.
Mind you, the anxiety is being felt by others than those
who have always been concerned about our growing
addiction to alcoholic beverages.
It is not the 'blue-noses' this time.

"It is the doctors, the sociologists, the educators, the law-
enforcement people, the employers who see its effects in
absenteeism,
    people like them who are really worried.

"And I predict that the United States, in the next ten years,
will have to do something about the problem, unless we
are to face a moral collapse with health and economic im-
plication.

"Incidentally, don't you think it funny that here in Washington—the one place in the country where we need clear

154

heads, steady nerves, and sound judgment for great decisions—more hard liquor is consumed than in any other city in the land?

"I can't say that it would be any sin for me to drink that glass of champagne.
No, but I know I shall not be able to speak with authority on that whole question, unless I myself have absolutely refused to compromise.
That's the reason why I won't touch it."

"I see your point all right," said the steel magnate, "but it seems like a high price to pay just for handing out a little advice across your desk."

"A high price? . . . Perhaps.
I suppose it really boils down to the question of how much we care about other people and about the future of our country."

"Of course I must admit," Mr Jones replied, "that I've never been much for religion, never could see how it could affect my life one way or the other.
Preachers' talk usually sounds like theological gibberish to me."
He paused . . . "Say, though, if you really think things in this country are that bad, what's the answer?
What can we do about it?"

"There's only one answer that I know of—God . . .
People like you and me becoming personally acquainted with Him.
When a man cultivates a personal friendship with the Chief, there's no life too much of a mess for Him to straighten

out—and keep straightened out—
  no problem He can't handle."

"I'm a hard-boiled sinner, parson, but somehow I'd like to
hear more.
How about having lunch with me sometime—say Tuesday?"

The minister pulled his little engagement calendar out of
his breast pocket . . . "Tuesday? . . . Tuesday it is".

So began a series of events that led a big business man to
Christ—that utterly and completely changed his life.

Our country is full of Joneses,
and they all have problems of one kind or another.
The Church has always contended that God can solve these
problems through the individual's personal fellowship with
a living Lord.

Let's put the question bluntly, as bluntly as Mr Jones
would put it. Is Christ really alive today, in this twentieth
century?
I don't mean can we treasure His words,
  or try to follow His example,
    or imagine Him?
I mean can we actually meet Him,
  commune with Him,
    ask His help for our everyday affairs?

The Gospel writers say "yes".
A host of men and women down the ages say "yes".
The Church says "yes".

The Church, you see, rests its unshakable conviction that

156

fellowship of that kind with a living Lord is possible, squarely on the fact of the Resurrection.

Now you may say that you believe in the Resurrection. But "belief", as the New Testament writers use that word, implies more than intellectual assent.
It is a belief which becomes a deep inner knowing—a certainty . . .
     a belief which reaches past the mind to the heart . . .
        a belief which flows directly into action.
Do you believe in the Resurrection *like that?*

A young woman, through a difficulty in her life, became aware of her need for Christ and for His help.
She also became aware—for the first time—of the fact that her soul was starving.
She was spiritually undernourished—hungry.

This woman began to rise an hour earlier in the morning, in order to find quietness and to read her Bible.
She discovered for herself the vitality of the Scriptures,
     their ability to nourish the human spirit.

Then one morning, two verses seemed to leap from the page, as if written in fire.
They seemed written just for her:
        "You search the scriptures, because you think that
        in them you have eternal life . . . yet you refuse to
        come to me that you may have life". (JOHN 5 : 39, 40)

Suddenly, the young woman realized her mistake.
She had been feasting her soul reading *about* Jesus.
But Jesus—the Risen Lord—was there in her quiet room, and she had been ignoring *Him.*

157

It was at that moment that the Resurrection became a fact of that woman's experience.

Do you believe in the Resurrection like *that*?

Perhaps you too, would like to feel Christ as real as that in your life.
You would like to find His plan for you—where you fit in.
You do want to feel, when you pray, that you are really talking to Him—not just carrying on a monologue.
You are willing to admit that you are by no means satisfied with the way your life is going.
That being so, you might ask me,
    "Then, where do I begin?
      What do I do?"

Those are valid questions and deserve a thoughtful answer. It is noteworthy that when certain individuals came to Jesus asking, "Master, what shall I do to inherit eternal life?" He did not say, "Well, pray, and read the Scriptures a little each day, and go to church".

As a matter of fact what He did do was to put His finger on the one great stumbling block in the seeker's life.
"Get rid of that", He might say—"your love of money and material security. That's cutting you off from God. When you have got rid of your materialism, then you will know the next step to take."

So let me try to indicate, as simply and plainly as I can, where one must begin and what one must do, in order to get started in this Christian life.

What I am going to say applies, of course, only to those

who are honestly seeking to find out.
If your interest in Christianity expresses itself only on Easter
 or only on Sunday mornings . . .
if you are a commuter into religion for two hours a week . . .
then this sermon is not for you.

First, if you are going to invite Christ to make Himself known to you—to reveal Himself and His plan—
 you've got to clean house before you invite Him in.

Fortunately this house-cleaning can be done rather as a chore, with no particular emotion, and it will be real and successful just the same.

Suppose for several days in succession—
 preferably at the same time each day—
you go to some quiet place where you can be alone and uninterrupted. Take a pencil and piece of paper with you. Ask God to show you any unconfessed and unforgiven sins out of your past, including those half-forgotten memories which you have pushed down into your subconscious mind.

Don't be afraid of the word "sin".
It's a sturdy, old-fashioned word.
It's an honest word.

You can be quite methodical about this.
Go as far back into your childhood as you can remember.
Have you been hanging on to resentments?
No matter how ill-used you have been . . .
 no matter how justified the resentment seems to you . . .
it is a sin and will have to be confessed as such.

L

These are the very emotions which cut you off from God . . .
which keep Him from seeming real to you.

If a memory is uncomfortable to recall, you will undoubtedly
find some unconfessed and unresolved wrong connected
with it.
At your request, Christ will go back over your past with you.
He will make you dig up all the things that you have
buried . . .
the things you tried to forget.
This is because He knows that it is necessary for you to get
your past straightened out, before your present and your
future can be made straight.

Then you take your list, all the things of which you are
ashamed, and you claim for yourself that wonderful promise
that

"If we confess our sins, He is faithful and just to
forgive us our sins, and to cleanse us from all un-
righteousness", (I JOHN 1 : 9)
and
"As far as the east is from the west, so far hath He
removed our transgressions from us". (PSALM 103 : 12).

When every uncomfortable memory has been confessed
before Christ, He will keep His promise and remove those
sins completely.
He will take away the feelings of guilt and shame.
He will make you feel clean again on the inside.
And you may then tear up or burn your list—and by the
grace of God, begin life anew.

This is where psychiatrists and psychoanalysts fail adequately

to minister to the needs of people.
They too, can go back to where things lie buried in the past.

They can make you dig them up,
    acknowledge them
  and face them—
but they have no healing ministry.

They cannot forgive.
    They cannot pronounce the word of absolution.
      They cannot remove the feeling of remorse and guilt.
        They are not God—It is not theirs to forgive.

Only Jesus Christ can speak the words that bring peace
to the harassed human heart:
      "Go in peace. Thy faith hath saved thee.
      Go—and sin no more".

Then you will have to keep in touch with Christ every day.
If you were anxious to get to know a human friend, you
would want to spend time in his presence.
So it is in cultivating Christ's friendship.

Perhaps in the beginning, you will have to make yourself
set aside a certain amount of time each day to talk with Him
    and to listen to Him.
But after a bit, you'll find that you can't do without that
time each day. It will mean too much to you to give it up.

Just as you have to nourish your body every day,
    so you need to nourish your spirit each day.

You will find that you have had some very wrong ideas
about God.

Perhaps you have been thinking of Him as a slave-driver—
    stern,
   demanding
  severe.
Instead, you will come to know Him as He is . . .
    a kind
    loving
   Heavenly Father
who is far more anxious to give you of His riches than you
are to ask for them.

Then you will have to make Christ the Lord of your own
life. That means that you must promise Him to make His
will supreme in your life, as truly as is the case with any
man conscripted into the army of his country.
Why is this necessary?

Let me illustrate it this way . . .
Suppose you needed medical help; you went to a physician,
and asked him to take your case. But suppose you told
this doctor, "I cannot really promise to do what you suggest
in my case. If your instructions please me, I'll obey them.
But if not—well, I'll do what I please . . ."

The physician probably would refuse to try to help such a
headstrong patient.
   Just so it is with God.
     He can guide us only if we are willing to be guided.
      Our self-will ties His hands.
        We cannot pick and choose the areas of our
willingness to obey.

The next step is to cultivate the fellowship of like-minded
Christians who, like yourself, are letting

God run their lives,
>   finding out what is God's plan for them,
>   and who are trying to do what He wants them to do.

This is where the Church comes in—
>   or should come in.
This is the real fellowship of believers, you see, not just a theological term, but a precious fellowship that will mean everything to you.

When people are really in earnest about this thing, they love to talk about it, and to help one another in their discipleship with Christ.
It was this fellowship that spread the Gospel in the beginning. This is the sort of thing that founded the Church. Why, this *was* the Church in the first century.

For, you remember, they had no buildings,
>   no organs
>   no organisation
no hymn books
none of the things we have today . . .
But they had fellowship with Christ . . .
>   They knew that He was with them . . .
>   They had the Holy Spirit . . .
>   and they had each other.

Until you have given yourself to such a fellowship, you are fooling yourself in believing that you have given yourself to Christ.
The Church, you see, is Christ's body on earth.
He planned the Kingdom of God, so that there is no such thing as a "lone wolf" Christian.

You will find that you can go only so far—and no further—
by yourself.

You need the fellowship.
   The fellowship needs you.
And as you give yourself to serve it,
   you, yourself, will be served.
Vistas will open up that would not be possible,
   if you tried to go it alone.

A Christian is not a man who is trying to *do* something.
   He is a man who has *received* something . . .
      a man to whom something has happened . . .
and who simply cannot keep it to himself.

Christianity is not something to be attained.
It is something to be obtained.
And here it is—
   ready and waiting for you this very day.

And yet, you must not expect any cut and dried formula or
set of rules about how to become a Christian, or how to
feel the reality of God's presence in your life.

It's not like the recipe for baking a cake.

It's more like being born—
   or falling in love.
It's a process—
   a growing thing—
      unfolding,
         continuing.

You don't arrive all at once—

But you do get on the right road—
  and then keep going.

I have tried to be practical and specific.
  I have indicated how you must begin.
    Are you willing to take these first steps?

There are fellow-travellers who have already started on the
road.
  They are happy.
    They are the happiest people I know . . .

Their lives are full,
    rich,
  abundant.
They make mistakes.
Of course they do—
  and they are the first to admit them.

They are not perfect—and they never will be, as long as
they are in this life.
But they are finding it fun to be Christians.
It's a great adventure.
They are living—gloriously alive.

How about it?
  Are you willing to take these first steps?
    When?
What's wrong with now?

Christ has been waiting for you—
How much longer are you going to keep Him waiting?

Prayer

Our Father, we are beginning to understand at last that the things that are wrong with our world are the sum total of all the things that are wrong with us as individuals. Thou hast made us after Thine image, and our hearts can find no rest until they rest in Thee.

We are too Christian really to enjoy sinning and too fond of sinning really to enjoy Christianity. Most of us know perfectly well what we ought to do; our trouble is that we do not want to do it. Thy help is our only hope. Make us want to do what is right, and give us the ability to do it.

In the name of Christ our Lord. AMEN.

There is beauty in homely things which
many people have never seen. For instance,
do you know
Sunlight through a jar of beach-plum jelly;
  A rainbow in soapsuds in dishwater;
An egg yolk in a blue bowl;
  White ruffled curtains sifting moonlight;
The colour of cranberry glass;
  A little cottage with blue shutters;
Crimson roses in an old stone crock;
  The smell of newly baked bread;
Candlelight on old brass;
  The soft brown of a cocker's eyes?

From LETTER TO A MOTHER

Keepers Of The Springs

ONCE UPON A TIME, a certain town grew up at the foot of a mountain range. It was sheltered in the lee of the protecting heights, so that the wind that shuddered at the doors and flung handfuls of sleet against the window-panes was a wind whose fury was spent.

High up in the hills, a strange and quiet forest dweller took it upon himself to be the Keeper of the Springs.

He patrolled the hills and wherever he found a spring, he cleaned its brown pool of silt and fallen leaves, of mud and mould
    and took away from the spring all foreign matter, so that the water which bubbled up through the sand ran down clean and cold and pure.

It leaped sparkling over rocks and dropped joyously in crystal cascades until, swollen by other streams, it became a river of life to the busy town.

Millwheels were whirled by its rush.
    Gardens were refreshed by its waters.
        Fountains threw it like diamonds into the air.
            Swans sailed on its limpid surface
and children laughed as they played on its banks in the sunshine.

169

But the City Council was a group of hard-headed, hard-boiled business men. They scanned the civic budget and found in it the salary of a Keeper of the Springs.

Said the Keeper of the Purse: "Why should we pay this romance ranger? We never see him; he is not necessary to our town's work life. If we build a reservoir just above the town, we can dispense with his services and save his salary".

Therefore, the City Council voted to dispense with the unnecessary cost of a Keeper of the Springs, and to build a cement reservoir.

So the Keeper of the Springs no longer visited the brown pools but watched from the heights while they built the reservoir.

When it was finished, it soon filled up with water, to be sure, but the water did not seem to be the same.
It did not seem to be as clean, and a green scum soon befouled its stagnant surface.

There were constant troubles with the delicate machinery of the mills, for it was often clogged with slime, and the swans found another home above the town.

At last, an epidemic raged, and the clammy, yellow fingers of sickness reached into every home in every street and lane.

The City Council met again. Sorrowfully, it faced the city's plight, and frankly it acknowledged the mistake of the dismissal of the Keeper of the Springs.

They sought him out in his hermit hut high in the hills, and

begged him to return to his former joyous labour.
Gladly he agreed, and began once more to make his rounds.

It was not long until pure water came lilting down under
tunnels of ferns and mosses and to sparkle in the cleansed
reservoir.

Millwheels turned again as of old.
   Stenches disappeared.
     Sickness waned
and convalescent children playing in the sun laughed again
because the swans had come back.

Do not think me fanciful
   too imaginative
     or too extravagant in my language
when I say that I think of women, and particularly of our
mothers, as Keepers of the Springs. The phrase, while poetic,
is true and descriptive.
We feel its warmth . . .
   its softening influence . . .
and however forgetful we have been . . .
however much we have taken for granted life's precious
gifts we are conscious of wistful memories that surge out of
the past—
   the sweet
     tender
       poignant fragrances of love.

Nothing that has been said
   nothing that could be said
     or that ever will be said,
would be eloquent enough, expressive enough, or adequate

to make articulate that peculiar emotion we feel to our mothers.

So I shall make my tribute a plea for Keepers of the Springs, who will be faithful to their tasks.

There never has been a time when there was a greater need for Keepers of the Springs,
or when there were more polluted springs to be cleansed.
If the home fails, the country is doomed. The breakdown of home life and influence will mark the breakdown of the nation.

If the Keepers of the Springs desert their posts or are unfaithful to their responsibilities the future outlook of this country is black indeed.

This generation needs Keepers of the Springs who will be courageous enough to cleanse the springs that have been polluted.

It is not an easy task—nor is it a popular one, but it must be done for the sake of the children, and the young women of today must do it.

The emancipation of womanhood began with Christianity, and it ends with Christianity.
It had its beginning one night nineteen hundred years ago when there came to a woman named Mary a vision and a message from Heaven.

She saw the rifted clouds of glory
    and the hidden battlements of heaven.
She heard an angelic annunciation of the almost incredible

news that she of all the women on earth . . .
   of all the Marys in history . . .
was to be the only one who should ever wear entwined the
red rose of maternity and the white rose of virginity.

It was told her—and all Keepers of the Springs know how
such messages come—that she should be the mother of the
Saviour of the world.

It was nineteen hundred years ago "when Jesus Himself a
baby deigned to be and bathed in baby tears His deity" . . .
and on that night, when that tiny Child lay in the straw of
Bethlehem, began the emancipation of womanhood.

When He grew up and began to teach the way of life, He
ushered woman into a new place in human relations. He
accorded her a new dignity and crowned her with a new
glory, so that wherever the Christian evangel has gone for
nineteen centuries, the daughters of Mary have been
   respected
     revered
       remembered
        and loved,
for men have recognized that womanhood is a sacred and a
noble thing, that women are of finer clay . . .
are more in touch with the angels of God and have the
noblest function that life affords.

Wherever Christianity has spread, for nineteen hundred
years men have bowed and adored.

It remained for the twentieth century,
   in the name of progress
     in the name of tolerance

in the name of broadmindedness
in the name of freedom
to pull her down from her throne and try to make her like a
man.

She wanted equality. For nineteen hundred years she had
not been equal—she had been superior.
But now, they said, she wanted equality, and in order to
obtain it, she had to step down.

And so it is, that in the name of broadminded tolerance a
man's vices have now become a woman's.
Twentieth century tolerance has won for woman
the right to become intoxicated
the right to have an alcoholic breath
the right to smoke
to work like a man
to act like a man—
for is she not man's equal?

Today they call it "progress" . . .
but tomorrow—oh, you Keepers of the Springs, they must
be made to see that it is not progress.

No nation has ever made any progress in a downward
direction.
No people ever became great by lowering their standards.
No people ever became good by adopting a looser morality.

It is not progress when the moral tone is lower than it was.
It is not progress when purity is not as sweet.
It is not progress when womanhood has lost its fragrance.
Whatever else it is, it is not progress!

174

We need Keepers of the Springs who will realize that what is socially correct may not be morally right.

Our country needs today women who will lead us back to an old-fashioned morality
  to old-fashioned decency
    to old-fashioned purity and sweetness
for the sake of the next generation, if for no other reason.

This generation has seen an entirely new type of womanhood emerge from the bewildering confusion of our time.
We have in the United States today a higher standard of living than in any other country, or at any other time in the world's history.

We have more automobiles, more picture shows,
  more telephones, more money,
    more swing bands, more radios,
      more television sets, more night clubs,
        more crime, and more divorce
than any other nation in the world.

Modern mothers want their children to enjoy the advantages of this new day.
They want them, if possible, to have a college diploma to hang on their bedroom wall,
and what many of them regard as equally important—a bid to a fraternity or a sorority.

They are desperately anxious that their daughters will be popular, although the price of this popularity may not be considered until it is too late.

In short, they want their children to succeed, but the usual

M

175

definition of success, in keeping with the trend of our day, is largely materialistic.

The result of all this is that the modern child is brought up in a decent
cultured
comfortable
but thoroughly irreligious home.

All around us, living in the very shadow of our large churches and beautiful cathedrals, children are growing up without a particle of religious training or influence.

The parents of such children have usually completely given up the search for religious moorings.
At first, they probably had some sort of vague idealism as to what their children should be taught.

They recall something of the religious instruction received when they were children, and they feel that something like that ought to be passed on to the children of today, but they can't do it,
because the simple truth is that they have nothing to give.
Our modern broadmindedness has taken religious education out of the day schools.
Our modern way of living and our modern irreligion have taken it out of the homes.

There remains only one place where it may be obtained,
and that is in the Sunday School,
but it is no longer fashionable to attend Sunday School.

The result is that there is very little religious education, and parents who lack it themselves are not able to give it to their children—so it is a case of "the blind leading the blind", and both children and parents will almost invariably end up in the ditch of uncertainty and irreligion.

As you think of your own mother, remembering her with love and gratitude—in wishful yearning
   or lonely longing . . .
I am quite sure that the memories that warm and soften your heart are not at all like the memories the children of today will have . . .

For you are, no doubt, remembering the smell of the starch in your mother's apron
   or the smell of a newly ironed blouse
      the smell of newly baked bread
         the fragrance of the violets she had pinned on her breast.

It would be such a pity if all that one could remember would be the aroma of toasted tobacco
   or nicotine
and the offensive odour of beer on the breath!

The challenge to twentieth century motherhood is as old as motherhood itself.
Although the average American mother has advantages that pioneer women never knew—material advantages
      education
      culture
advances made by science and medicine
although the modern mother knows a great deal more about sterilization, diets, health, calories, germs, drugs, medicines, and vitamins, than her mother did, there is one subject about

177

which she does not know as much—
  and that is God.

The modern challenge to motherhood is the eternal challenge—that of being godly women.
The very phrase sounds strange in our ears. We never hear it now.

We hear about every other kind of women—
  beautiful women,
    smart women,
      sophisticated women,
        career women,
          talented women,
            divorced women,
but so seldom do we hear of a godly woman—or of a godly man either, for that matter.
I believe women come nearer fulfilling their God-given function in the home than anywhere else.

It is a much nobler thing to be a good wife than to be Miss America.

It is a greater achievement to establish a Christian home than it is to produce a second-rate novel filled with filth.

It is a far, far better thing in the realm of morals to be old-fashioned than to be ultra modern.

The world has enough women who know how to hold their cocktails
    who have lost all their illusions
  and their faith.
The world has enough women who know how to be smart.

It needs women who are willing to be simple.
The world has enough women who know how to be brilliant.
It needs some who will be brave.
The world has enough women who are popular.
It needs more who are pure.
We need women, and men too, who would rather be morally right than socially correct.

Let us not fool ourselves—without Christianity
    without Christian education
  without the principles of Christ
inculcated into young life, we are simply rearing pagans.

Physically, they will be perfect.
Intellectually, they will be brilliant.
But spiritually, they will be pagan.
Let us not fool ourselves.

The school is making no attempt to teach the principles of Christ.
The Church alone cannot do it.
They can never be taught to a child unless the mother herself knows them and practises them every day.

If you have no prayer life yourself it is rather a useless gesture to make your child say his prayers every night.

If you never enter a church it is rather futile to send your child to Sunday School.

If you make a practice of telling social lies it will be difficult to teach your child to be truthful.
If you say cutting things about your neighbours and about

fellow members in the church it will be hard for your child to learn the meaning of kindness.

The twentieth century challenge to motherhood—when it is all boiled down—is that mothers will have an experience of God . . . a reality which they can pass on to their children. For the newest of the sciences is beginning to realize, after a study of the teachings of Christ from the standpoint of psychology, that only as human beings discover and follow these inexorable spiritual laws will they find the happiness and contentment which we all seek.

A minister tells of going to a hospital to visit a mother whose first child had been born.
She was distinctly a modern girl.
Her home was about average for young married people.

"When I came into the room she was propped up in bed writing.
" 'Come in', she said, smiling. 'I'm in the midst of house-cleaning and I want your help.'

"I had never heard of a woman house-cleaning while in a hospital bed. Her smile was contagious—she seemed to have found a new and jolly idea.
" 'I've had a wonderful chance to think here', she began, 'and it may help me to get things straightened out in my mind if I can talk to you.'
"She put down her pencil and pad, and folded her hands. Then she took a long breath and started:
" 'Ever since I was a little girl, I hated any sort of restraint. I always wanted to be free. When I finished high school, I took a business course and got a job—not because I needed the money—but because I wanted to be on my own.

" 'Before Joe and I were married, we used to say that we would not be slaves to each other. And after we married our apartment became headquarters for a crowd just like us. We weren't really bad—but we did just what we pleased.'

"She stopped for a minute and smiled ruefully.
" 'God didn't mean much to us—we ignored Him. None of us wanted children—or we thought we didn't. And when I knew I was going to have a baby I was afraid.'

"She stopped again and looked puzzled. 'Isn't it funny, the things you used to think?'
"She had almost forgotten I was there—she was speaking to the old girl she had been before her great adventure.

"Then remembering me suddenly—she went on: 'Where was I? Oh, yes, well, things are different now. I'm not free any more and I don't want to be. And the first thing I must do is to clean house.'

"Here she picked up the sheet of paper lying on the counterpane. 'That's my house-cleaning list. You see, when I take Betty home from the hospital with me—our apartment will be her home—not just mine and Joe's.

" 'And it isn't fit for her now. Certain things will have to go—for Betty's sake. And I've got to house-clean my heart and mind. I'm not just myself—I'm Betty's mother.
And that means I need God. I can't do my job without Him. Won't you pray for Betty and me and Joe,
    and for our new home?'

"And I saw in her all the mothers of today—mothers in tiny apartments and on lonely farms . . .

Mothers in great houses and in suburban cottages who are meeting the age-old challenge—'that of bringing their children to the love and knowledge of God'.

"And I seemed to see our Saviour—with His arms full of children of far-away Judea—saying to that mother and to all mothers—the old invitation so much needed in these times:
    'Suffer the little children to come
    unto me and forbid them not, for of
    such is the kingdom of God'."

I believe that this generation of young people has courage enough to face the challenging future.

I believe that their idealism is not dead. I believe that they have the same bravery and the same devotion to the things worth while that their grandmothers had.

I have every confidence that they are anxious to preserve the best of our heritage, and God knows if we lose it here in this country it is forever gone.

I believe that the women of today will not be unmindful of their responsibilities; that is why I have dared to speak so honestly.

Keepers of the Springs, we salute you!

Prayer

*Our Father, remove from us the sophis-
tication of our age and the scepticism that
has come, like frost, to blight our faith and
to make it weak. Bring us back to a faith
that makes great and strong, a faith that
enables us to love and to live, the faith by
which we are triumphant, and the faith by
which alone we can walk with Thee. We
pray for a return of that simple faith, that
old-fashioned trust in God, that made strong
and great the homes of our ancestors who
built this good land and who in building left
us our heritage.*

*In the strong name of Jesus, our Lord,
we make this prayer.* AMEN.

The Church has in her keeping the secrets of prayer and meditation and communion with the risen Christ, but perhaps she has kept them in the icebox of orthodoxy.

From HUNGRY SHEEP

The Problem Of Falling Rocks [11]

DRIVING ALONG the highways that run through the mountains, you may have noticed the frequency of signs that read:
"Beware of falling rocks".
I have seen them many times and have often wondered why they did not say, "Beware of fallen rocks", for I do not know what one could do about rocks that were in the act of falling as one drove along.

Now this is a hazard of driving along these highways that no precautions can avoid.
Your rate of speed has nothing to do with it . . .
  nor the way you handle your car
    nor the condition of your tyres.
It makes no difference whether you are a good driver or a bad driver, the hazard is there and there is nothing you can do about it.

It is typical of those troubles in life which no caution can avoid, and which have nothing to do with one's conduct, be it good or bad.
The insurance people call them "Acts of God".
When they come
  they come
    and that's that.

This is not fatalism, but a recognition that God has set up in this world He has made certain natural laws that govern inanimate things.

The question I ask you to consider is what should be our attitude toward these troubles that we can do nothing to prevent?
The commonest attitude is one of worry, for this is the most common and widespread of the transgressions that mark our inconsistency as Christians.

I suppose the cartoon character, "The Timid Soul", meeting one of these signs along the highway, would peer anxiously above his shoulders, and seeing the overhanging boulders would turn his car around and drive back.

But suppose he decided to drive on and risk it.
He might drive very carefully and worry all the time, lest one of these huge rocks break loose and come crashing down upon him and his new car.
But what good would his worrying do him?
It wouldn't hold the rock up there; neither would it jar it loose.

The worrying of the driver has no effect upon the rock, but it has a tremendous effect on the driver.

People have never fully realized just how destructive a thing worry is.
It truly plays havoc with one's life.
    It ruins digestion.
        It causes stomach ulcers.
            It interferes with sound sleep and forces us to face another day unrested and irritable.

It shortens our tempers and makes us snap at the members
of our family.

Anxiety and tension, which are twins, bring on heart disease
   high blood pressure
      and nervous disorders.

Ask any doctor, and he will tell you that the patient who is
apprehensive retards his own recuperation.

Hard work, even overwork, never killed anybody.
It is not the amount of work we do, or have to do, that harms
us. It is the strain or tension caused by our anxiety over the
work that counts.

We would live longer, and do more and better work, if we
could bring ourselves to the philosophy of an old Negro I
read about, who said:
         "When I works, I works hard:
      When I sets, I sets loose;
   When I worries, I goes to sleep".

Would that sleep would overtake us when we begin to worry.
We would be healthier.
   We would live longer.
      Our dispositions would be sweeter.
We would be nicer to know and easier to live with.

Jesus had a lot to say about this very thing.
In the sixth chapter of Matthew's Gospel you will find quite
a full quotation on this theme in the Sermon on the Mount.
Jesus said: . . . "take no thought for the morrow"—that is,
no anxious, troubled thought—

Or we might well say, "Don't worry about tomorrow"—for
that is precisely the meaning of His words.

"Which of you, by taking thought, can add one cubit unto
his stature?"
You can't suddenly make yourself a foot taller than you are.
That is one of the things of life you have to accept.
Fretting about your lack of inches will not increase them.

If you borrow trouble from tomorrow, anticipate the difficulties that you see, or think you see ahead, are you the
better able to cope with them?

Can you, by worrying, keep something unpleasant from
happening?
　　Do you soften the blow
　　　　ease the burden
　　　　　　or lessen the pain?
Of course not, but you stand a good chance of reducing your
ability to take it.

I want to make a distinction between thoughtful consideration on the one hand, and the useless fretting on the other
　　that destroys peace of mind
　　　　takes away appetite
　　　　　　and leaves a person sleepless and miserable.
It is this latter useless fretting that I have in mind.

The futility of it was illustrated perfectly in the case of our
little boy.
The year he was in kindergarten he enjoyed it very much, for
it was nearly all play.
Then when he moved up into the first grade,

he was shocked to discover that he had to learn things—
  In short, he had to think
    and had less time to play.
He was very unhappy about it,
and as he wrestled with the problem of learning the letters
of the alphabet
  how to read them
    and how to write them
his mind was troubled.

Many a time, in the midst of his play,
his lower lip would tremble,
and he would burst into tears, crying as if his heart would
break.

Having been told that he had twelve years of study before
him, and then possibly four years of college after that, he was
most miserable.

He would confess between his sobs that he was worrying
about going to college, and what he would do when he got
there.

Now that seems to us ridiculous—
but not any more so than some of the things we grown-ups
worry about.
Of course, if you are *not* a Christian you have plenty to worry
about.

But if you are a Christian
  if you are a child of God
then your worrying is not only futile,
  it is sinful.

For worry, to the Christian, is really a sin.

When Christ turns the searchlight of His penetrating insight
and decisive intellect upon worry,
He defines it in a very simple way.
He sees it as nothing more or less than lack of trust in God.

With regard to the rocks that may fall upon us, and in these
days of the atom bomb they are heavy and sinister, the only
happy way to deal with them is the way of faith—
faith in the purposes of God
   faith in the presence of God
      faith in the promises of God
         faith in the power of God to deliver us in any trouble.

Only when we have faith can we be free from fear.
If you are afraid, then we must suspect that you have no
faith in God.

A good deal of the strain and tension of modern life is due
to our unwillingness to accept situations that are beyond
our control. Christians must be realists as well as idealists,
and Christ was both.
There was never clearer realism than is to be found in the
teachings of Jesus.

When we resist things we cannot change, then we have
strain inside—inner tension—and that is what causes the
trouble.

We plan a vacation trip and then somebody gets sick, and
we have to postpone it . . .
but inside we are filled with self-pity and resentment.
The train is late, and we miss our connection, and we sit and

fume trying to push the train along the track,
  and by glaring at our watch try to stop the hands.

The maid does not show up some morning, and the household schedule is thrown out of gear.
Frustration and resentment send us banging and slamming
through the house.

You have a lot to do in the office, but you discover that your
secretary is sick and not able to work,
  and you fume, and your blood pressure mounts,
    and you glare at the gremlin that sits on your desk and
    grins at your annoyance.

Common sense tells you that the best thing to do is to accept
what you cannot help and make such adjustments as are
necessary.
An uncompromising attitude changes nothing but yourself,
and the change is never for the better.

We have to learn to cooperate with the inevitable.
We'd better.
Man proposes, but God disposes.
There are so many things in life beyond our control that
he is wise who recognizes the fact and who says:
  "God willing, I will do this or that . . . "
This is not mock piety, but clear recognition of life's con-
tingencies, and our helplessness in certain situations.

The rocks will fall.
We don't know when, and we cannot find out for sure.

Worrying about it, fearing it, does not help.
Life must go on, and so must we.

But we can go on without strain.

We all have had the experience of how in our lives there are
stretches of uneventful days, and then, generally without
warning, some crisis is sprung upon us.

You may at any moment be plunged into some great calamity
that brings your dreams crashing around you . . .
    takes the song out of your life
        and makes your heart so sore that you wonder why it
        doesn't break.

It would not be so bad if troubles sent us warning.
If we received night letters telling of approaching difficulties,
at least we might be prepared—although with most of them
there would be little we could do.

At least the shock would not be so great.
But troubles do not do that.
They do not come marching down the road—out in the
open.
No, they wait in ambush, and they spring out at us when
we least expect them.

Most of us live sunny lives of ease and comfort and hear
only rumours of pain and distress.
Tales of human terror are blown to us very faintly from
another world that seems unreal
   distant
      having nothing to do with us.

As long as the sun shines for us we find life quite a happy
thing.
But when the sun is hidden, and the dark clouds gather, we

have no right to whine or cry out as if we were being ill-treated to some injustice that was invented solely for our distress.

We know already that at this very moment a great many people are in real trouble.
We know it in our minds, but not in our hearts.
Shakespeare said that it is not difficult to bear other people's toothache.
The surprising thing is that each of us considers his own trouble to be important and worthy of sympathy, until he learns of the troubles of others.
Then he realizes that perhaps he is not so badly off after all.

Troubles are cannibals in the sense that the big troubles eat up the little ones.
Every pastor knows full well that in his congregation there are people who keep going with real trouble, so that he can be forgiven if sometimes he seems lacking in sympathy with the people who are merely petulant.

I never feel so unworthy and so indicted in my own grumblings, as when I learn of the troubles of others.

Suppose you were bereaved suddenly,
and so many expressions of love and gratitude were left unsaid.
Suppose you were left alone now,
and then you thought of so much that love could have said, and gratitude could have done.
Just suppose that happened to you!

One of the things Christ definitely promised us was trouble.

"In the world ye shall have tribulation", He said.
But we must never forget that He added:
    "But be of good cheer" . . . or, in other words,
    "Cheer up . . . I have overcome the world".

Now, when trouble comes, when the rocks do fall, it will not help to reject faith altogether, and fling away in revolt from all that you once believed.

For in God's name where will you go?
    To what else will you cling?
What would you substitute for Christian faith?

Just because you may not understand what has happened to
    you or why it should have come
is no reason why you should throw it all away.

If Christ is right, then there is a loving purpose in it all . . .
even though our tear-filled eyes cannot see it.

If Christ has not lied to us, then there is a reason behind even the darkest providence.
There must be a reason, for God rules;
    and the reason must be good, for God is good.
It must be the under side of love, for God is a God of love.
When you are in the sunshine you may believe it.
But when you are in the shadow you must believe it, for you have nothing else.

The promises of the Scriptures are not mere pious hopes or sanctified guesses.
They are more than sentimental words to be printed on decorated cards for Sunday School children.

They are eternal verities.
They are true.
There is no perhaps about them.

How does the prophet know that God will neither leave us
nor forsake us?
How does the psalmist know that the broken-hearted and
the afflicted will be comforted?

Because they themselves had dark days and lonely nights.
That's why!
Because they themselves had gone through it.

These Scripture truths are fragrant flowers that their own
fingers plucked from the gardens of human experience.
Sometimes the thorns pricked them, but they held on to the
flowers.

"I will not leave you comfortless", Christ says.
And only those whose hearts have been left desolate . . .
only those who have needed comforting . . .
needed it desperately . . .
know how true that promise is.

Christ does not leave us comfortless, but we have to be in
dire need of comfort to know the truth of His promise.

It is in times of calamity . . .
in days and nights of sorrow and trouble
that the presence
the sufficiency
and the sympathy of God grow very sure and very
wonderful.

Then we find out that the grace of God is sufficient for all our needs
   for every problem
      and for every difficulty
for every broken heart, and for every human sorrow.

It is in times of bereavement that one begins to understand the meaning of immortality.
You think today, as the sun streams in golden shafts through the window and birds sing of spring, you think that you believe it.

But wait until you stand at the edge of an open grave . . .
Then you will know what it means to believe it.

You will not then be interested in chattering about immortality . . .
   or gossiping about the theories of the hereafter . . .
You will know . . .
deep down in your own heart, you will know.

We have such pagan ideas about death—most of us—not at all Christian or in keeping with the revelation we have in the Scriptures.

We are wrong who haunt the cemetery as if to feel the presence of loved ones who are not there, if Christ has told us the truth!
   We have our eyes wrongly focused.
   We do not understand.

Our tears are selfish, for we are self-centred—self-absorbed.
We keep thinking of what it means to us.
We reflect how much we miss the departed,

and we weep because we begrudge their going.
 We wish they had stayed on with us awhile . . .
  We wish things had gone on as they were.
We resent the change, somehow, never thinking what it
must mean to them that are gone.

In the New Testament we hear little of the families with that
aching gap,
very few pictures of mourners huddled together sitting
silently in their homes . . . weeping . . .
No, but you do hear a great deal about the Father's house of
many mansions . . . and the angels.

Let us therefore act like believers,
live like Christians so that we can die like Christians . . .
 with songs and rejoicing.
That is the true Christian attitude.

Those we love are with the Lord, we believe,
and the Lord has promised to be with us,
 never to leave us nor forsake us:
  "Behold I am with you always".

Well, if they are with Him,
 and He is with us . . .
  they cannot be far away.

It is not true to sing—or even think—of Heaven as being far
away.
It is no distant land
 no alien shore
but near us—very close.
It gets nearer as we grow older.

As more and more of our friends and loved ones go home,
our thoughts and expectations turn ahead to the time when
we shall all meet again in the new life . . .
       in the other room
    never again to part.

But meanwhile, between now and the time when the bell
shall toll for us, we still have a pilgrim way to travel.
It may be smooth or rough, we cannot tell.
Troubles may come—troubles will come.

How shall we deal with them when they do come?

It is a truism that "all God's chillun got trouble", and the
only thing, after all, that sets God's children apart from
other people is what they do with trouble.

I think the Christian treatment of trouble is splendidly illustrated by the oyster, into whose shell one day there comes
a tiny grain of sand.

By some strange circumstance, this tiny piece of quartz has
entered into the shell of the oyster and there like an alien
thing
    an intruder
       a cruel, unfeeling catastrophe
imposes pain
    distress
       and presents a very real problem.
What shall the oyster do?

Well, there are several courses open.
The oyster could, as so many men and women have done in

times of adversity and trouble, openly rebel against the sovereign providences of God.

The oyster, metaphorically speaking, could shake a fist in God's face and complain bitterly:
"Why should this have to happen to me?
Why should I suffer so?
What have I done to deserve this?

"With all the billions of oyster shells up and down the seaboard, why in the name of higher mathematics did this grain of sand have to come into my shell?"

The oyster could conclude:
"There is no justice.
All this talk of a God of love and mercy is not true.
Now, since this calamity has overtaken me, I'll throw away all the faith I ever had. It doesn't do any good anyway".

Yes, the oyster could say that.
So many men and women have in times of trouble.
But the oyster doesn't!

Or the oyster could say—again like some men and women when adversity strikes . . .
"It can't be true!
It isn't true.
I must not permit myself to believe it".

The oyster could say—as some of our very best people today are trying to say in the face of cruel circumstance:
"There is no such thing as pain. This grain of sand doesn't make me uncomfortable, and I'm not going to

allow my mind to think of unreality.

"There is no such thing as pain. It is an error of the mind, and I must, therefore, project my thoughts on positive planes of beauty
    truth
      goodness
and if I fill my mind with such thoughts, then I shall know that pain is unreal."

But the oyster doesn't do that.
There is another attitude the oyster could adopt—a very commendable one—one that calls for a lot of fortitude and courage and determination.

The oyster could say:
    "Now that this hard calamity has overtaken me
      this thing that hurts and cuts and stabs
        this enemy that bruises and bleeds
now that this has come upon me, I must endure to the end.
I must show them all that I can take it, and I won't give in.
    I will hold on if it kills me.
    I must remember that the darkest hour is just before the dawn."

Now, there is something noble in that,
    something praiseworthy in that attitude.
But the oyster does not do that,
because the oyster is at one and the same time a realist as well as an idealist.
There is no point in trying to deny the reality that tortures every nerve, so the oyster doesn't try.

In spite of all the denial, nothing can change the fact that the grain of sand is there.

Nor would grumbling or rebelling do any good,
for after all the protests and complaints, the grain of sand would still be there.

No, the oyster recognizes the presence of the grim intruder, and right away begins to do something.
Slowly and patiently, with infinite care, the oyster builds upon the grain of sand—layer upon layer of a plastic, milky substance that covers each sharp corner and coats every cutting edge . . .
    and gradually . . . slowly . . .
        by and by a pearl is made . . .
           a thing of wondrous beauty wrapped around trouble.
The oyster has learned—by the will of God—to turn grains of sand into pearls
    cruel misfortunes into blessings . . . pain and distress into beauty.

And that is the lesson that we are to learn along this pilgrim way.
The grace of God, which is sufficient, will enable us to make of our troubles the pearls they can become.
It is no mere figure of speech.
It is something more than a simile to say that one enters Heaven through pearly gates.

One enters into the presence of the Lord through gates bedecked with pearls,
and every pearl—a trouble
        a pain
      a heartache

a misfortune
which, by the grace of God, has been changed into a
beautiful, lovely thing.

No wonder they speak of pearly gates!

Prayer

Our Father, give us the faith to believe that it is possible for us to live victoriously even in the midst of dangerous opportunity that we call crisis. Help us to see that there is something better than patient endurance or keeping a stiff upper lip, and that whistling in the dark is not really bravery.

Trusting in Thee, may we have the faith that goes singing in the rain, knowing that all things work together for good to them that love thee. Through Jesus Christ, our Lord. AMEN.

We need a faith that is as real as fire
. . . and prayer as real as potatoes.

THE HEART OF THE CREED

The Touch Of Faith

" And his disciples said unto him Thou seest the
multitude thronging thee, and sayest, thou, Who touched
me?" (MARK 5 : 31)

THAT IS AN ELECTRIFYING QUESTION when you realize
who asked it, and under what circumstances. You
cannot escape the thrill of it—the tingle of excitement that grips you when you think of Christ stopping in
response to the touch of a poor nameless woman.

The words of this question are not cold
         abstract
      inanimate
   dead words.

They do not form a hook on which one could hang theories
or finely spun philosophies. No, they are too vital for that.
They march into the vestibule of your heart and knock on
the door.

They suggest all kinds of daring thoughts to your weak
faith.
They are like sparks falling into dry grass.

The setting of this text is a vivid picture—colourful, appealing, and of absorbing interest.

The incident takes place in a city street. It is a narrow
twisted street packed with a crowd of gesticulating, excited

205

people, surging past its bazaars and pavement stalls with all the noise and confusion of an eastern market place.

A murmur of conversation grows louder as the procession pushes its way through the narrow street. There is a sound like the chanting of some mysterious dirge that frequently rises to an excited crescendo. Here and there a voice rises distinctly out of the medley in what might have been a prayer; but it is lost in crackling laughter, rudely interrupted and drowned in the barking of dogs and the argument and discussion of a crowd that loves to talk.

They are caught up in the infection of curiosity, and walking along in their very midst, wedged in the tightly packed procession is Someone. . . .

It is His face that will hold your gaze—and will haunt you long after the sun has gone down, and the purple night, cool and starlit, has stilled every noise in the city, while only the Syrian stars wink unsleeping.

One is aware of that face even in such a crowd. Having once seen it, one sees it everywhere, for it is a haunting face—an expression that will not fade . . . eyes whose fires never die out . . . a face that lingers in memory. Farmers were to see it as they followed the swaying plough, and fishermen were to watch it dancing on the sun-flecked water.

This One who walks like a king is named Jesus. They called Him the Nazarene or the Galilean. He called Himself the Son of man.

The common people speak of Him softly, with deep affection, such as the shepherds know, who carry the little lambs in their bosoms.

The beggars whisper His name in the streets as they pass, and the children may be heard singing about Him. His name has been breathed in prayer and whispered at night under the stars. He is known to the diseased, the human flotsam and jetsam that shuffles in and out of the towns and drifts hopelessly along the dusty highways of human misery.

His fame has trickled down to the streets of forgotten men, has seeped into the shadowed refuges of the unremembered women. It is Jesus of Nazareth.

Any outcast could tell you of Him. There are women whose lives have been changed who could tell you of Him—but not without tears. There are silent men—walking strangely as if unaccustomed to it—who speak of Him with lights in their eyes.

It is Jesus whom they are crowding to see. They want to look on His face to see the quality of His expression that seems to promise so much to the weary and the heavy-laden; that look that seems to offer healing of mind and soul and body;
    forgiveness of sin;
      another chance—a beginning again.
His look seemed to sing of tomorrow—a new tomorrow—
in which there should be no more pain
                  no more suffering
               nor persecution
            nor cruelty
          nor hunger
        nor neglect
      nor disillusionments
    nor broken promises
  nor death.

o

At the request of one Jairus, a ruler of the synagogue, He is on His way to restore to complete health a little girl.

He is on a mission of restoration, and the crowd is following Him in order to see Him perform this miracle.

Speculation is rife.
  Opinion is divided.
    There is argument and excited discussion.

Some are declaring that He can do it; others are doubtful.
Some frankly say the attempt is bound to fail.

However, their curiosity is aroused, and it promises to be an interesting experiment.

There is in the crowd another face—the face of a woman. Strange that it should be so noticeable—yet not strange, for it is a face that portrays great depth of human emotion.

There is so much in it—pale, pinched, and wan. Great lines of suffering mar its beauty and sweetness, and even now her lips are drawn in a thin line of agony.
The face is streaked with pain.
Her body is racked with acute suffering.

Who is she? Well, some say her name is Martha
  and some say Veronica.
Tradition gives her various names, but I cannot tell who she was.

It does not matter.
Is it not enough that she was a woman in pain?

Call her Martha . . . or Mary . . . or Margaret . . .
    or mother . . . or sister . . . or wife.

She is typical of countless cases of endless pain and suffering.
For twelve years she had suffered
    and twelve years is a long time!

Her malady seems to have been a pernicious haemorrhage
    or a form of bleeding cancer.
She had gone to many physicians and was no better—
    but rather worse.

She had spent all that she had, and every new day was
another hopeless dawn. Every sunset was stained with the
blood of her pain.

She is typical of human despair—not only physical despair
but spiritual despair as well. For her the world could offer
no healing—so she represents all the people who look everywhere for peace of mind and heart—for hope and comfort—
and find none.
She represents them all—whatever their wants
        their fears
    their hopes
    their pains.

For her apparently, there was no relief, no human aid. Hers
was a hopeless case—incurable!

After twelve years of treatment—she was no better. What
would *we* do?

We would probably send her to some home for incurables,

and visiting clergymen would be embarrassed to know what to say to her.

Now, this woman had heard of the Great Teacher,
   of His wonderful works.
She had heard the lepers talk and them that had been blind from birth and now had thrown away their sticks, and looked around them with eyes that flashed or filled with tears as they spoke His name.

She had heard what He had done for others.
Surely He had power to bring into the haven of health the lost explorers of the vast treasuries of pain!

Surely, He had power to lift from the dust of disease the flowers whose stems had been crushed or withered in the mildews of human misery!

As this thought burned itself into her mind her faith was curiously stirred as it wrestled in the birth-throes of a great resolve.

It was daring—fantastic, perhaps.
Her heart thumped
   but it was worth trying.
    It could only fail
and she was no stranger to failure.

There came to the woman the assurance that if she could but touch Him—even only the hem of His garment—she would be healed of her awful malady.

Cannot you imagine her nervous reasoning?

"Touch Him . . . yes . . . just to touch Him—
There would be no harm in that!

"I do not think He will harm me . . .
They say He is so kind
    and gentle
        so full of sympathy.

"Besides, here is my great chance.
    He is coming this way
        soon He will be gone.
Why not touch Him as He passes?

"On the head!—no, that would be irreverent!
I would not dare!
Well, on the hand!—no, that would be too familiar!
But there cannot be any harm in touching His robes as He
passes.

"It would be enough—just to touch the border of His
robes. I *must* touch Him. I *must* get some of that power."

Thus reasoning, she pushes her way through the crowd
and with the pertinacity of despair she struggles in that
dense throng
    nearer and nearer
        pushing and crushing.
People get in the way—not knowing her need.

Now she is desperate. He must not pass so near and yet so
far away. Was she to lose this opportunity?
    She must touch him.

Now just a little farther. He is drawing nearer. Now she can

211

almost reach Him—another moment—at last just as He passes, she is able to reach out her hand, and with the tip of her finger touch His robe.

It was enough! She had actually touched the Great Doctor!

With a trembling finger she had touched Him with the touch of a mighty faith! Like an electric shock there surged back into the shrunken veins
    the panting lungs
   the withered muscles
  and the bloodless flesh
the rich glow of health and vitality.
Once again a body had been redeemed and given life.

She had touched Him with secret and trembling haste and thrilled with the change that had come to her, she retreated back into the crowd
unnoticed, she thought.

No one had noticed her—
   no one—but Christ!

Recognizing the one magnetic touch of faith amid the pressure of the crowd, He stopped and asked that *terrific* question:
"Who *touched* me?"

The question seemed absurd to those who heard it.

Impatiently, brusquely, almost with sarcasm, the disciples asked: "How should we know?
There are hundreds of people here—pushing all about you.
Look at the crowd—

and yet you ask 'Who touched me?' "

But, looking around Him, Christ stood still—His kind, but searching, glance fell at last on the face of the woman who had done it.
His gaze held hers. Something passed between them, and she told Him her story while His eyes were fixed upon her; His eyes gave her confidence. They seemed to promise all that she desired. Her fear disappeared.

Then He answered her:
  not in scorn at her action
    not in resentment
      not in anger at her presumption
    not in ridicule at her faith
  not in indignation at her audacity
but in the sympathetic tones of understanding love

"Daughter, thy faith hath made thee whole.
Go in peace . . . and be healed of thy plague."

That is the record. These are the facts.
        It is a matter of history.

She had no money—only faith.
  She did not meet Him in a house of worship.
    She met Him on the street.
She had no private audience with the Lord.
  She touched Him in a crowd.

She touched Him in faith—in desperate believing faith and He stopped!
The touch of one anonymous woman in a crowd halted the

213

Lord of glory. *That is the glorious truth of this incident. She touched Him. So can we.*

Let us take it into our apathetic hearts
  let its glorious significance thrill our jaded souls.

The human touch has the power to arrest God.
Yes, to stop Him
  to halt Him
    to make Him aware of your problems
      your pain
        your petition.

Oh, you say, "That's impossible. God is not interested in me. What does He care what happens to me—one tiny individual in all this creation?
Who am I—or what am I that God should take special notice of me?"
Well, there is the record.
  There you have it in black and white
that, stopped by the touch of a sick woman, He turned about—
  He who conquered death
    He who defeated Satan
      He whom all the legions of hell cannot stop
        He who is King of kings.
He stopped just because a sick and nameless woman touched the hem of His garment.

We need to touch Him—O how much we need to touch Him!

Most of us are thronging Him—just like the crowd . . .
It is easy to throng the Lord and never touch Him.
A great many people in the churches, and perhaps **a great**

many outside the churches, are thronging Jesus
   seeking Him
      coming close to Him
         but never actually touching Him.

In this matter of eternal importance, coming close is not
enough.
It is like missing a train . . .
   You may miss it by one minute—and that's pretty close—
but you have lost the train . . .
   It is gone, and you are left behind.

Thronging saves nobody.
   Coming near to Jesus will not bring healing.
   We have to touch Him for ourselves.

One can feel close in the crowd without touching the Lord.
And that is exactly the trouble with most of us. We are
following the crowd
   thronging the Lord
but not many of us are actually in touch with the Master.

And because we are not in touch, there is no vitality in our
spiritual life.
There is no thrill in our prayers
   no tingle of contact with the infinite resources
      no flush of reality about our religion.
Because we are out of touch with the Lord,
   we are lost in the crowd
      have become separated from the Master.

We preach the Immanence of God.
Our creeds set forth our belief that the Lord is with us
     near us
   in this very place.

215

The Old Book records for us some amazing promises
  some startling assurances if we would
    only believe them.

He promised that we should have power
    power—to do amazing things
  grace—to do unnatural things, such as
to harbour no grudges and to forgive those who hurt us
  to love even those who treat us unjustly or unkindly
    to pray for those who give us pain and grieve us
      to confess our own private and secret sins
        to try to make right situations that have been
wrong, even if it means humbling ourselves, swallowing
our pride, and risking a snub or a slight.
We can have grace to do these things, and we know perfectly well that it takes a lot of grace to do them!

He Who made these promises is here with us now.

But you may ask: "How can I touch Christ?"
It was one thing for that woman long ago, for she saw Him
with her eyes, and could touch Him with her fingers.

She heard His voice,
  saw the sunlight dance on His hair.

He was in the flesh then, and she could touch Him.

How can I, today, touch Him with the same results?

Some of you may seek healing of body or mind or of soul.
Some of you may seek guidance on some problem.

216

Some of you need faith to stand up under the tensions and suspenses of life.

Some of you seek forgiveness and a new beginning.

All of us need to touch Christ for some reason or other.

As the Church offers this wonderful new life—this peace of mind and heart—this healing of mind and soul and body in Christ's name—perhaps she ought more and more to give instructions with her soul medicine.

You are justified in looking for directions on the lid
  or some instructions for taking
    a manual of operation.

Perhaps I can make some suggestions which will be helpful.

First, give God a chance. Take your problem, whatever it may be, to Him in prayer. Tell Him all about it—just as if He didn't know a thing. In the telling be absolutely honest and sincere. Hold nothing back.

Our minds are sometimes shocked when we permit our hearts to spill over, but it is good for our souls when we do.

If we would only have the courage to take a good look at our motives for doing certain things we might discover something about ourselves that would melt away our pride and soften our hearts so that God could do something with us and for us.

Then the second step is to believe that God will hear you. Remember that He heard the poor woman who only touched the hem of His garment. Believe with all your faith that He cares what happens to you. You must believe that. You can't doubt it when you look at the cross.

Next, you must be willing to wait patiently for the Lord. He does not answer every prayer on Sunday afternoon. You may have to wait until Friday. But wait. God is never in a hurry.

Then when He speaks to you—as He will—do what He tells you. He may not tell you audibly. You may not hear your voices—as did Joan of Arc. You may not see any writing in the sky and have any unusual experience. God *could*, if He wanted, send you messages in that way, but that is not His usual method.

It generally comes through your own conscience—a sort of growing conviction that such and such a course of action is the one He wants you to take. Or it may be given you in the advice of friends of sound judgment—those who love you most.

God speaks sometimes through our circumstances and guides us, closing doors as well as opening them.

He will let you know what you must do, and what you must be.
He is waiting for you to touch Him.
The hand of faith is enough. Your trembling fingers can reach Him as He passes.
Reach out your faith—touch Him.
He will not ask, "Who touched me?"
He will know.

Prayer

Teach us, O Lord, the disciplines of patience for we find that to wait is often harder than to work.

When we wait upon Thee we shall not be ashamed, but shall renew our strength.

May we be willing to stop our feverish activities and listen to what Thou hast to say, that our prayers shall not be the sending of night letters, but conversations with God.

This we ask in Jesus' name. AMEN.